PLEMS

THORNY PROBLEMS

A seasonal collection of gardening queries and answers from The *Daily Telegraph's* much-loved columnist

Helen Yemm

WINDSOR
PARAGON

First published 2011
by Simon & Schuster
This Large Print edition published 2011
by AudioGO Ltd
by arrangement with
Simon & Schuster (UK) Ltd

Hardcover ISBN: 978 1 445 85888 3
Softcover   ISBN: 978 1 445 85889 0

British Library Cataloguing in Publication Data available

Printed and bound in Great Britain by
MPG Books Group Limited

Contents

WINTER

To begin with: some truly practical gardening and something that I hope will make you smile. The following brief exchange was overheard (by me) at a local garden centre.

'Hello, mate. Do you sell trees?'
'Yes indeed we do, sir. What sort of tree had you got in mind?'
'Oh, I dunno. Something that will fit in the car.'

Introduction

This slim volume is a distillation of the best (or should that be the worst?) of Thorny Problems, the letters page of *The Daily Telegraph*'s Saturday Gardening section, inspired and fuelled entirely by the gardening problems and anxieties of real gardeners. My fervent wish is that it should find a place by the bed, in the shed (or in the loo) of all those who have enjoyed Thorny Problems over the years—and hopefully a lot more people besides— and that it will help sort out some of the most common gardening frustrations that trouble us all.

When deciding how to deal with the almost overwhelming amount of material that is the result of several years of Thorny Problems, we decided that the most useful way to do it would be to make it into a month-by-month practical book. Within its pages you will find all sorts of gardening bits and bobs you never thought you didn't know, and I have tried to ensure that my 'rough guides'— on clematis, rose and hydrangea pruning, for example, on composting, and on the worst weeds —are inserted into the seasons in which they are most relevant.

For those who are unfamiliar with Thorny Problems, perhaps I should explain how it all came about. (Although *Telegraph* readers are familiar with my take on things by now, I am not a well-known horticultural Big Name.)

At the start of the new century I wrote a little book *Gardening in Your Nightie*—now out of print. I ran informal gardening courses from my home and it was loosely based on the notes I gave my students, most of them thirty- and forty-something first-time keen-as-mustard Londoners, seeking unintimidating advice on all the basics, as well as a little inspiration and encouragement from someone who had actually been there and done it—nursed the backache and wrecked the nails.

Something in *Nightie* caught the eye of *The Telegraph*'s then gardening editor and within months I found myself writing regularly for the Saturday Gardening section. When I took over the letters column, I was asked, tentatively, if I would also be prepared to deal with readers' problems via email. Thus Thorny Problems was born. Over the past few years, the page has developed a life of its own and is as 'live', informal and interactive as it is possible to be, given the limitations of newspaper production.

Throughout this time, my own life has also changed considerably. Gardening has been a passion for years, but never in a month of Sundays did I ever expect to become a writer. I had, however, presented a couple of gardening programmes for the BBC (*Gardening from Scratch*). I had turned my back on London and taken on a large unruly patch of land around an old East Sussex farmhouse. My learning experiences—successes and failures, needless to say—of creating borders out of nothing, making and maintaining ponds, planting trees, and taming overgrown hedges, as well as prettifying a threadbare orchard, thus fed the first few years of Thorny Problems. When I wasn't up to my elbows in the garden, I was picking my way through an endless stream of *Telegraph* readers' queries:

toiling over long and friendly letters, or standing in my muddy boots by a kitchen worktop on which was perched my overworked laptop. The garden flourished somehow, and was open for the National Gardens Scheme and featured in the *Good Gardens Guide*. For me they were hectic but extremely creative years, in every sense. By 2005, if asked, I would probably have described myself as a writer who gardened—no longer a gardener who wrote.

All this was just as well, since in that year my life imploded and I found—with no warning—that I would have to leave my beloved home and garden and start all over again in a very much smaller place. But my move managed somehow to give Thorny Problems a new lease of life. In my old house I had enjoyed acres of space in which to play with plants and had compost bins the size of most people's garden sheds; and I had, I suspect, gone a bit 'grand'. My new, smaller horizons are perhaps more in keeping with 'normal' gardening on this increasingly crowded island, and the garden I have since made is much more manageable. And yet I have all that 'big garden' experience and know-how tucked away up top and am able to draw on it for ever.

Enough. Enjoy the book.

Helen Yemm
March 2011

Spring

March

READING BETWEEN THE LINES

we garden writers, seemingly in collusion with the dreamers who produce the copy in plant catalogues, constantly over-use superlatives that make our favourite plants sound lip-smackingly irresistible. We don't mean to mislead exactly, and most canny gardeners know the score. For 'vivid blue' read, as often as not, 'purple', for fashionable 'black' read at best 'dark red' or worst 'wet-mud-coloured'. Is the colour of delphinium 'Astolat' ever described as 'a dull, dirty pinkish mauve'? Who admits that the 'intoxicating' scent of winter-flowering sarcococca is also 'nauseating when you get it indoors'? Well they should—and furthermore those who describe *Jasminum beesianum* as a must-have with scented red flowers should be strung up by the thumbs. Only when it has legged-it messily up to the gutters will it produce a few pinhead-sized, deeply insignificant flowers whose scent is practically indiscernible.

I think most gardeners, even those that do 'instant', have now got enough savvy to avoid plants such as Russian vine—as well as the tediously messy 'evergreen' honeysuckle (*Lonicera japonica*) and even dear old *Clematis montana*— unless they have infinite space in which to let them romp about. But the small print of the labels of less obvious baddies should ring alarm bells in our heads: 'vigorous', 'can be invasive'. Instead they seem to act more as a come-on to the eternally

3

plant-hungry, who choose to interpret them slightly differently. For 'vigorous' we think, 'yippee, even I won't be able to kill *that*', while 'can be invasive' means 'great, even if I only plant one, my border will look instantly stuffed'.

Plants that are frequently sold to the unsuspecting as useful border plants, but which will run completely amok underground, include superficially pretty charmers such as *Achillea ptarmica* 'The Pearl' and feathery-leaved, lime-flowered *Euphorbia cyparissias*. In the wrong place, which rapidly becomes everywhere, they can be as much of a nightmare as ground elder, travelling into the hearts of other plants and reducing a border to a confused mess within a couple of years. Others that spread nuisance seedlings everywhere when your back is turned include that large muddy pink *Geranium oxonianum* 'Claridge Druce', plus fennel and *Alchemilla mollis* (both of which you can almost, but not quite, forgive since they are so lovely) and the plain green-leaved sisyrinchium.

So my advice to beginners and to anyone planting a new garden is this: learn to recognise all those marketing euphemisms. It may be easier said than done, but try to read catalogues and the writings of plant addicts with a pinch of salt and do research before buying permanent garden plants, preferably asking someone who actually grows that which takes your fancy about its general growth habit, pruning requirements and so on.

Be wary, too, of well-meaning friends and relations, who in addition to giving masses of really helpful advice, may off-load all sorts of horticultural riff-raff and do-too-wells without turning a hair. Always ask yourself—and them—

4

why they are being so generous. And if these benefactors come semi-clean and tell you that they had 'too much' of this or that, then don't imagine that the plant you are taking on will behave any differently in your garden than it did in theirs. Dump your excess thugs on the compost heap, not on your friends.

As a postscript to the above, there is the tricky problem of 'inheritance' that many of us have to face... The previous owner of my house was seduced—twice—by the idea of a shrubby, scented winter-flowering honeysuckle (*Lonicera fragrantissima* or a close relation thereof). As a consequence there is (or was until one Sunday) one almost blocking my back door and another almost blocking my front door. This shrub is a bore in my view, and not worth the considerable space it takes up. Its leaves are as dull as forsythia, its growth angular and rampant and it flowers briefly in February when it is so cold that to experience even the mildest olfactory frisson you would have to stuff the flowers right up your nose. Furthermore, the flower scent does not even, unlike daphne or the aforementioned sickly-cocca, 'take off' when picked for a delicious winter posy. Maybe space could be found for it in a large shrubbery, but to find two so strategically placed was a bush too far. So I chopped one out from between paving stones and my house wall, and put most of it though my shredder. At least it had a useful role to play as compost.

And what about replacing it? The small piece of east-facing wall—about 9 × 5ft (2.7 × 1.5m), at right angles to French doors leading from my little office on to my paved area—will be clad in small-

5

squared trellis, up which will grow a real favourite of mine about which I bang on a lot, namely *Trachelospermum jasminoides* (see also July, page 114); an easy, neat, not particularly rampant evergreen twiner that will produce hundreds, yes *hundreds*, of starry white gloriously jasmine-scented flowers between May and September. Honestly it will.

THE WHITE IDEA

I am having trouble tracking down a supplier of white forget-me-not seeds. Do you know where I can find them? I would like to grow them with white tulips as part of an all-white-flowered front garden. Also, have you any ideas for any out of the ordinary white-flowering plants, preferably with a long season?
Margaret, Fordingbridge, Hampshire

Firstly, the seed company Chiltern Seeds sells many flowering plants by single colour rather than in the usual dizzy mixtures, including white myosotis (forget-me-not).

I'd also recommend seeds of tall white *Cosmos bipinnatus* 'Purity' (quite different—loftier and waftier—from the more stocky 'bedder' 'Sonata') and of the old-fashioned, really smelly, white tobacco plant *Nicotiana affinis*.

Have you thought, however, about plants with grey foliage and those with lime-green flowers, both of which enhance an all-white colour scheme? Plants to conjure with that give weeks of value include old cottage-garden thug *Alchemilla mollis* (lady's mantle), which is easy to control if you shear off the old flowers promptly, after which it does it all over again. Felty-grey-leaved *Lychnis coronaria* 'Alba' (often called dusty miller) is a short-lived but long-season perennial that self-seeds usefully. In sheltered gardens shrubby *Artemisia* 'Powis Castle' or ground-hugging *A. stelleriana* (both cut back each spring after last frosts) could provide weeks of white-ish foliage interest. The same goes for another filigree-leaved white 'filler' that is slightly less hardy: *Senecio viravira*. I first saw this in the famous white garden at Sissinghurst.

And do you contemplate climbers? I was bowled over recently at the sight of a white-flowered scrambling climber, *Solanum laxum* 'Album', which is certainly hardy in your part of the world. Friends here in Sussex have one flowering its heart out around their front door, even after very cold weather. It had been at it non-stop since early summer, they tell me.

PRUNING HYDRANGEAS

Throughout the year I get complaining letters about hydrangeas that flower pathetically, or are congested, twisted, miserable messes. I sense that most of your woes can be put down to haphazard pruning. There is the enthusiastic hacker who strongly suspects he has gone wrong somewhere because all that is left after pruning a once glorious mop-head are a few unpromising-looking

7

stumps—and his wife is jumping up and down threatening to bin the loppers. Then there is the timid tweaker, who despite good intentions just nipped out, nipped off the flower heads and nipped back in again to warm up, because she can't quite work out how to take the bull by the horns. Where pruning is concerned gardeners are a predictable lot. Maybe what is needed are some basic instructions, with no unhelpful step-by-step drawings of perfect specimens. So here it is—a mug's guide to hydrangea pruning.

The most commonly grown hydrangeas fall, broadly speaking, into one of two categories.

Hydrangea × macrophylla are the mop-heads and lacecaps. Being slightly tender, they should be tackled in late spring: the end of March or even early April in cold areas. If you start by squatting down, looking at the undercarriage of each bush, you will see that there are several different generations of shoots massed together. The aim is, quite simply, to preserve the youngest shoots with their tips intact, trim down and tidy up the middle-aged ones and remove the oldest completely. This will ensure you get plenty of large flower heads and will also create space for the coming season's new growth. Really neglected bushes will probably have a lot of completely dead wood in them that can be snapped out by hand before you start the real business, which should go something like this.

All the new straight growth that grew from the base last season but did not flower should be left completely alone, with shoot tips intact. All shoots that grew from the base the previous year and whose tips carried single flower heads last summer should be shortened down by about 1ft (30cm) to a pair of fat flower buds. (Leaf buds are generally slimmer and pointed; flower buds are fatter and rounded.) These fat buds will develop into two short branchlets that will carry flowers in summer. Shoots that were pruned like this last spring and which branched and flowered last summer can be cut out from the base. Anything much older (i.e. thicker, browner and multi-branched) should also be cut out at the base. Once you have pruned like this the job should be far simpler in subsequent years—and you will be much more confident.

The other common category is the *Hydrangea paniculata* and *H. arborescens* groups—with names such as 'Brussels Lace' and the much-loved 'Annabelle'. Once the bushes are mature and have developed a sturdy, woody base, they are easier to deal with. Enthusiastic hackers will be in their element, and can safely be let loose on them. In March treat these hydrangeas much as you would any other substantial late summer-flowering shrubs, such as *Buddleja davidii*, and prune stems down to a pair of buds on a fairly sparse framework around 2ft (60cm) high. These buds will become strong shoots that carry flowers on their tips.

All hydrangeas appreciate a post-pruning dose of general fertiliser, lightly forked in around their bases, followed by a dollop of leaf mould, composted bark or home-made compost.

And while we're on the subject of pruning, we gardeners know there are all sorts of ways of cutting things back. You can hack blindly, tweak ineffectively or do it 'by the book'. Precisely *which* book is up for discussion and it appears that (as I suspected) we all have a different favourite. There

9

are occasions, however, when we may simply be forced to undertake what I call 'first aid pruning': cutting things back at a less than ideal time perhaps, harder than is advisable maybe, in order to regain control, see what is what, and start to move a choked-up garden forward.

I got to grips with pruning the easy way—under the guidance of my father (a plant physiologist) when he was renovating a massively overgrown garden years ago. He was quite brutal with his loppers but quietly confident, a man of few words. 'C.R.B. it will S.O.F.T.B.' (Cut it Right Back it will Shoot Out From The Bottom) was his frequent advice to me, a querulous novice with a pruning saw. He was generally right—particularly about roses—and it was a lesson well learned. After all, those intricate pruning rules and guidelines (which he also explained to me) are about ensuring seamless continuation of growth and optimum flowering, and generally fail to highlight the fact that it is in the nature of all plants to survive and grow. If you chop off their heads, more often than not mature woody plants will defiantly sprout. They may look less than lovely and not flower for a year or more, depending on the severity and the timing of the operation, but they will eventually, perhaps very eventually, recover. Their subsequent brave re-growth can be pruned and manipulated anew.

BEE LIST SHRUBS

Has a whole generation of young gardeners gone slightly bananas? Seduced by alien exotica (bamboos, cannas and phormiums head the list), anything foreign-looking with big leaves or a bit of drama has been shoehorned en masse into the nation's sheltered back gardens. But things may be changing for the better, as we become more aware of the plight of our honey bees and scientists and beekeepers urge us to plant bee-friendly shrubs. Ten key bee-attractive shrubs have been given the thumbs up: ceanothus, heathers, thyme, lavender, hebe, iberis, escallonia, sage, pyracantha and broom. These are distinctly un-exotic species and I'm hoping this is the start of the Great Flowering Shrub Revival, since to me they are the backbone of a balanced garden.

In my view there is no sight lovelier in a sunny summer garden than a massive lavender bush swaying under the sheer weight of tipsy, nectar-grazing bees. But there is more we can do to attract bees than plant a few more flowering shrubs. Bees are attracted to our gardens by sugar-laden nectar, the bee's main source of energy, and by the magic dust with which they pollinate our plants and which provides them with proteins and fat. Scientists like to dazzle us with other facts about bees. Did you know, for example, that they are attracted to flowers not just by colour but also

11

by fluorescent pigment, invisible to us, notably in flowers that only open late in the day (for example, *Mirabilis jalapa*, the four o'clock plant)? Or by iridescence—light-altering texture rather than colour (think about CDs)—in flowers such as tulips?

But let's forget about anything remotely scientific. As pleasure-gardeners what we really should be doing is simply cramming our gardens with flowers that not only attract bees and other pollinators, but also show them off so that we can just sit back in tranquil moments and watch them at work—probably as blood-pressure-lowering an activity as watching a tank of tropical fish in a dentist's waiting room. So my 'list' to attract bees is pretty much endless and includes just about everything with a flower, from abelia to zinnia. Consider adding plants to your garden with open, flat flowers, particularly those that can loosely be described as 'daisies'—kicking off the season with doronicum and progressing through the erigerons, via old-fashioned calendula and cosmos to gorgeous rudbeckias, and finally, as the shadows lengthen, to asters and heleniums. And just as important are the numerous pincushion-shaped flowers around which they love to congregate: monarda, the numerous scabious relations, sedums, verbenas, valerians and, best of all, echinops, teasels and cardoons.

A QUESTION OF WEIGHT

Mark writes to ask why it is that, if John Innes No 3 compost is sold as the ideal medium for potting trees and shrubs in permanent containers, so many gardeners (myself included) frequently recommend mixing a peat- or peat- substitute-based compost in with it. Can I please explain myself? he asks. Yes sir, indeed sir, I will sir.

John Innes No 3 compost, sold in bags by various compost companies, is a gritty, soil-based compost rich in nutrients. It is the nearest thing you can buy to rich garden soil, and of more reliable nutrient content than most bagged topsoils—thanks to the addition of the John Innes base fertiliser (two parts hoof and horn, i.e. nitrogen; two parts superphosphate; and one part potassium sulphate).

The only problems with it in containers are its weight and its ability to harden like rock and form a crusty top, making watering difficult. The addition of a small quantity (say, 25 per cent) of something 'softer' circumvents this problem.

I personally prefer using soil-based composts. In common with many gardeners, I find that lighter— perhaps cleaner—'multi-purpose' peat- or peat-substitute-based composts have their drawbacks. Once they have dried out they are hard to wet. This is particularly irksome in summer for containers of annuals (although there water-retaining products you can add to them, and some potting composts for containers are now sold already laced with them). I find that plants raised from seed (in John Innes Seed and Cutting Compost, aka No 1), or those that are potted on (into John Innes No 2) to be planted out eventually into garden soil, seem to do better than those started off in non-soil-based composts.

As always, there is no 'right' or 'wrong' to this, but I was asked to explain myself, so I have.

MAKE YOURSELF COMFREY

I have been offered some small comfrey plants by a neighbour who has found a big patch of it on his new allotment. How do you grow comfrey and how is it best used?
Maria, by email

Comfrey, beloved by organic gardeners because of the high potassium content of its leaves (two or three times that of farmyard manure), is extremely easy to grow. The most common variety is Russian comfrey—*Symphytum × uplandicum*—introduced into this country in the 1870s by a certain Henry Doubleday, a Quaker smallholder who subsequently became the founder of Garden Organic (formerly known as the Henry Doubleday Research Association, and more latterly the HDRA). A particularly tall, leafy, deep-rooted variety of *S. × uplandicum* rather curiously named 'Bocking 14' is the one that organic gardeners seek out. It grows well in the shade, does not spread by seed but it can nevertheless be invasive, so needs careful placing.

Comfrey leaves can be used in several ways. Early in the season the first crop of leaves can be cut, left to wilt and laid in a 2in

(5cm) deep layer at the bottom of trenches dug for main-crop potatoes, beans and so on. Further harvests can be made every few weeks and used to make comfrey concentrate—a potash-rich fertiliser for use around the garden. To make the concentrate you simply cram cut leaves into a large container that has a tap at the base. After a few days a black liquid can be drawn off and bottled and diluted as needed with 15 parts water. The resulting leaf slurry can finally be added to a compost heap. You can also make a weaker brew by steeping leaves in water in a lidded container or water butt, using 12lb (5.4kg) of leaves in a 20 gallon (90 litre) butt. However, this method is not for those with sensitive noses or small gardens, since the butt will smell like an open sewer every time you lift the lid or extract the liquid. Even if you fail to get to grips with all the steeping, brewing, bottling and diluting, comfrey leaves simply added to a compost heap act as a highly effective activator.

WAYWARD WINTER JASMINE

I cut down a really overgrown winter jasmine growing against the house wall three years ago, after it had finished flowering. It grew back with a vengeance and despite efforts with string and secateurs it is intent on having its own way. Would a trellis be a good idea? How should I prune and train it to get some sort of order out of it, without losing flowers?
Jackie, East Sussex

15

This is a plant that likes to think it is a climber, and indeed looks best trained up a wall, but makes absolutely no effort to get up there by itself. A trellis would be a good idea. Fixed with its horizontal ribs outermost, you can thread some of the arching stems up behind it at different heights and they will cascade forwards through it. This year, prune only the tips of the shoots you use as 'climbers', but cut the rest back as described below. It will start cascading in earnest next year. Every few years you may have to do a radical spring refurbishment with secateurs, removing unproductive woody shoots entirely. For this reason it may be sensible to fix the trellis so it can be easily removed from the wall. I have been known to hang trellis off a wall on large hooks, carefully placed to distribute the weight—it makes painting the wall and servicing climbers really easy.

Winter jasmine should always have tired shoots cut out after flowering (back to a pair of good buds on each). But if for practical reasons you need to keep it relatively compact, the new growth can be shortened with shears in June and it will shoot anew. However, if you prune later in the season, you run the risk of removing the best of next spring's flowering shoots.

WORM CASTS ON THE LAWN

Last summer we dug up and replaced our old lawn, using good-quality topsoil and turf. It looked wonderful, but now is being completely ruined by worm casts, which end up as flat muddy patches with no grass growing through—despite the fact that we haven't trodden on the lawn all winter. Is there anything we can do to stop this happening?
Linda, Cranleigh, Surrey

The worms under your lawn are clearly having a field day working their way through your new lawn—and the bad news is that, realistically, there is not an awful lot you can do about it. The potent worm-killing chemicals of yesteryear are no longer around. You can try to deter them temporarily by increasing the acidity of your soil, however. You can achieve this by spraying your lawn with a sulphur-based product such as Sulphurlawn. You will need to repeat the treatment regularly and it works best if you first 'tine' your lawn (remove plugs of soil with a special hollow-tined fork) or at least spike it deeply with a garden fork, and then top-dress it with a sandy turf dressing. Worms are, let us remember, essentially good for the garden and will, via their network of tunnels, be doing an excellent job of heaving organic debris underground to rot down, at the same time aerating the ground for you.

You say you have not been treading on the lawn much during the winter, but I do suggest that you get yourself a besom (witch's broom) or a rubber-tined rake and just sweep the worm casts lightly off the surface of the turf whenever you think about it during the next few weeks.

The good news is that while worms have a very irritating flurry of activity at this time of year, they calm down completely as the soil dries out and go down deeper underground for the summer. They will undoubtedly come up in the autumn for a repeat performance.

THE WRONG SORT OF WORM

The soil here in Spain is extremely dry and we hardly ever find worms in it. When we do—it is about as exciting as finding gold—we drop them in the compost bin. However, I have never noticed them multiply in there, even though we turn the compost regularly and water it. Are we doing something wrong? I have heard of wormeries, which I presume are a composting system of some sort. Are they sold commercially or can I improvise with an ordinary plastic container?
Dorothy, Alicante

How many readers can there be in Alicante, scurrying around their gardens looking for worms, I asked myself? But your questions provide an opportunity to correct a major misconception about our favourite garden friends (except when they are messing up our lawns with their casts—see opposite).

Earthworms—the most commonly found

18

are lob worms—prefer to muck around in cool, moist soil. As you have found, they are generally not much in evidence in dry soil but they surface and snap into action when conditions suit them best—spring and autumn in the UK. Dropping the odd earthworm into a warm and steamy compost heap in the hopes that it will somehow be beneficial is not a good idea. The poor old things will not survive for long and would be much better left in situ to generally churn around where they feel at home, aerating the soil as they do so.

The worms that really do the business in compost heaps (and in wormeries) are commonly known as 'reds', brandlings or tiger worms. They occur naturally close to the surface in damp woodland leaf litter and in the absence of predators they can (almost unbelievably) live about 15 years, breeding every two weeks or so. These are the worms that are supplied by the kilo by the companies that make wormeries—lidded containers with drainage holes for the copious liquid fertiliser that is the principal by-product—in which you can compost your vegetable kitchen waste. By all means improvise and build your own wormery. There is even a book—*Worms Eat My Garbage* by Mary Appelhof—that will tell you all you need to know.

WEEPING VINES

My husband cut back the young grapevine that he has decided to train across our west-facing garage wall, having previously let it get rather out of hand. The cut stems have been dripping profusely ever since. Will the vine bleed to death? Is there anything that can be done to stem the flow?
Liz, Worthing, West Sussex

I can read the panic between the lines of this one. The sap of the grapevine (*Vitis vinifera*)—and its ornamental cousins such as *Vitis coignetiae*—rises with extraordinary power in spring. When stems are accidentally cut, or if pruning is carried out a little too late, the stems invariably drip horribly. It absolutely goes against human nature to ignore weeping wounds but there is really nothing that can be done, and although the loss of sap does seem to slow the plant down a bit, it will be unlikely to suffer in the long run. Eventually the flow will slow down, the branch tips dry up and everything will return to normal. Cutting the vine stems in late summer (you may find you have to do this, just to get some of the growth out of your hair) is unlikely to result in such a flood, but your husband would do well to do most of his pruning in mid-winter in future, when he should cut back new growth to within a couple of buds of the new permanent framework of branches (only keeping such new growth as is needed to extend that

20

framework). At that time the whole plant should be completely dormant, and there should be no disasters.

DAPHNE IN TROUBLE

When I moved to France last year, my daughter bought me a **Daphne odora,** *which is now looking very sad. None of the flower buds opened and the lower leaves flopped, turned pale and all but two fell off. Is there anything I can do?*
J M, by email

It is not unusual for unhappy daphnes in the wrong place to drop leaves and look miserable around now. This is a subject close to my heart since I adore daphnes and have successfully grown *Daphne odora* in the past, but a new one in my care started to decline in the way you describe. However, having now seen for myself the conditions in which they grow in the wild I feel confident that I know the answer. On a trip to Nepal I walked through a forest of mighty rhododendrons over 7,000ft (2,133m) up in the Annapurna foothills. Surprisingly, as trees these rhododendrons were almost conical, and some must have been around 50ft (15m) tall. Their bare lower growth was festooned with all manner of epiphytes (orchids), moss and lichen, while the forest floor beneath rustled with a permanent blanket of barely rotted leaves from the evergreen canopy. Growing under the trees on the steep mountainside in this relatively cool, still gloom, protected from weather extremes and with roots kept moist by the thick leaf mulch, was a scrubby underworld of assorted leggy daphnes and close relations, as well as sarcococcas, mahonias, berberis—and, of course, plants I had never seen before in my life. They probably only received at most a couple of hours of sun each day.

Rather than leave its survival to chance, I think you would do well to move your unhappy daphne forthwith—it could well perk up and produce new leaves from the shoot tips. It may sound like a tall order, but try to replicate most of the conditions it would enjoy in the wild, namely a site that is protected from wind by other plants and partially shaded for some of the day, with leafy soil that neither gets waterlogged in the winter nor bone dry in the summer.

TRANSPLANTING SNOWDROPS

An email from Mrs M of Huddersfield caught my attention. Shocked at the price of little pots of snowdrops at her local garden centre this spring, she is inclined to accept the offer of her kindly neighbours, who say she can take some from the 'masses' that line their driveway. Are there any special tips, she asks, to give the transplantees the best chance of flowering next year?

Giving away snowdrops (and thus thinning out congested colonies) at this time of year is one of the nicest things an over-endowed gardener can do, since they transplant extremely well when they have just finished flowering. Mrs M should gratefully take whole spade-loads of bulbs if they are offered, right now, while the leaves are still green, taking the trouble to replant a few in the gaps she creates in her neighbours' colony. Once she gets them next door, instead of planting them lock, stock and barrel as they were dug up (which is a great temptation, since it avoids all the following fiddling around), she should gently shake the soil off them all, taking care not to damage the hair-like roots, and quickly plant them in small loose bundles (up to half a dozen bulbs in each), before they dry out. The snowdrops should be planted between 2–5in (5–12cm) deep in soil that has had a little bonemeal added to it, preferably watered into the planting holes, before the soil is gently firmed up around them. If they are to be planted in grass, she can simply remove small sections of turf, put in the bulbs with a sprinkling of fertiliser, water them and gently scatter with soil followed by the plug of turf. If she has to delay planting, she should wrap the snowdrop-y clods in newspaper and keep them damp, or heel them into a flowerbed temporarily.

The leaves of the transplanted snowdrops are unlikely to rally much after their disruption, and will just lie around looking rather messy for a few weeks as they gradually yellow, then brown, then fade away. During this time the bulbs should not be allowed to dry out. Foliar feeding with a soluble fertiliser would provide them with an extra fillip, but if they have been planted in grass, Mrs M should be aware that this will also green-up the turf and accelerate its rate of growth, which might look rather strange.

The groups of bulbs will look best if they are slightly random, rather than regimented, and will gradually expand over the years until they join up and Mrs M has her own 'mass' that she can, in turn, thin out and pass on to others.

FORGOTTEN BULBS

Mrs Wright is just one of several who have discovered bulbs that they forgot to plant, now merrily sprouting in bags. Can they be saved or should they be consigned to the compost heap? Plant them somewhere out of sight—all in a jumble if necessary. Put a stick in the soil next to them to indicate where they are—you may forget that, too, later on. They will flower, late and rather chaotically perhaps, after which you should foliar feed the leaves and let them die down completely. Lift and store the bulbs and REMEMBER TO PLANT THEM NEXT YEAR. On no account should they be put on the compost heap. If they are, they will come back to haunt you from the depths of the compost next year. I know these things...

A DIFFERENT JASMINE CHALLENGE

Incredulous but determined Jane M has bought herself one of those tiny flowering potted jasmines growing over a little metal hoop, having been assured by a rather smug acquaintance that this was how her own now massive and gloriously flowering 5ft (1.5m) plant started life. When hers has finished flowering, apart from re-potting it into something larger, what should she do to get it going?

The re-potting bit is important. Jane should choose a heavier pot, tapping off some of the old compost (which is undoubtedly a peat- or peat-substitute-based one) and using a soil-based compost—John Innes No 2. The old flowering shoots should be cut back and the wire replaced with something more robust, about 3ft (1m) high, to accommodate this summer's expected growth. New little shoots should already have started to grow from the jasmine's base, and these are the ones that Jane should train up and around the new support(s), and which will carry next year's flowers. Weekly feeding and a sojourn outside during June, July and August will be beneficial, or it can go into a greenhouse (doors open in summer) as mine does. I bring mine into the house and start to feed it with tomato food around Christmas and it is now a smother of flowers, the smell of which is almost overpowering. Also smug? *Moi*?

April

PETER'S FRIENDS

In my previous garden, buried deep beneath the boundary hedges, were three rabbit warrens. This area, a mere 50 miles from London—and frequently referred to as Wandsworth-in-the-Weald—is falling increasingly into the hands of what I call the New Farmers. They are all geared-up with snorting four-wheel drives and shiny, throbbing mowing machinery, but are, how shall I say, perhaps a bit too lax in the general land-management department. I rather suspect some of the newest arrivals, brought up on a wholesome diet of Beatrix Potter, are somewhat surprised to see rabbits running around without their blue jackets. In my view the only good rabbit is a braised one, and I have a fabulous recipe for rabbit with balsamic vinegar. But I digress... All of this is bad news for gardeners. As bold as brass, whole gangs of bob-tails cavort on grass verges in broad daylight, and hippety-hop around in gardens.

It took me several months to realise that it would be impossible to have a garden of any interest without completely excluding rabbits from at least part of it. Conveniently hidden behind internal hedges, I had a 3ft (1m) high barrier of chicken wire erected around about a quarter of the land. The bottom foot or so of this was buried under the turf not vertically, as you might instinctively think it should be, but horizontally.

The rabbits bob up to it, start to dig, and hit the wire with their claws and give up. The gates also had an overlay of chicken wire and I was absolutely neurotic about closing them at dusk each day.

To be on the safe side, outside the wire fence most newly planted shrubs and trees were caged for their first two years with cylinders of chicken wire (dark green hardly shows). Once they have made thick woody stems they will generally survive the odd investigatory nibble, although the lowest leaves, new base shoots and the shoot tips of any shrubs with weeping branches will always be vulnerable. Most damage is done in the spring, and while I concentrated on planting things that rabbits will leave alone, I protected the early growth of the odd rabbit herbaceous 'must have' (such as *Geranium pratense*) in the wild grassy areas with bamboo or chicken-wire cloches. The following brief list of flowering plants that rabbits dislike, or those that will recover from early spring munch-offs, is based on my own experience. I know from readers' letters that rabbit tastes are dependent on how hungry they are—and that they cannot be relied on to be consistent. My list is largely made up of plants that are considered suitable for growing in wild areas, a combination of which makes a lovely informal garden of sorts. I would never attempt to grow vegetables or set my sights on smart formal borders in a rabbit-infested garden—it would be too heartbreaking. Total exclusion has to be the best solution.

Spring bulbs: bluebells (and their tall relation, camassia), snowdrops, daffodils.

In damp areas: all members of the primula

28

family, soapwort, purple loosestrife, various irises, king cups.

Also: Joe Pye weed, achillea, foxgloves, all varieties of comfrey, ox-eye daisy, campion, knapweed, goat's rue, teasel, lychnis, marjoram, forget-me-not, hawkweed, some asters, cow parsley, alkanet, bugle, ferns, thick-leaved hostas.

GROWING SEDUMS ON A ROOF

I recently saw some clumps of succulent plants—presumably sedums and houseleeks—growing on the roof of an old building. I would like to have a go at doing this, and wonder if there is anything special you have to do when planting to make them 'stick'?
Amanda, by email

This is something I regret never having tried when I had an ancient house with an old tiled roof, and I fear that my Edwardian slate roof with its various flat-roof extensions just won't quite cut the mustard. I have a friend—gardener and writer Richard Bird—who has achieved some success on the old Kent peg tiles of his house, so I asked him if he had any tips.

Apparently you have to gather some cow pats and plaster them on the roof before you plant the sedums and houseleeks. The cow pats—presumably mixed (oh what fun) with a little peat and grit—are sufficiently sticky to bond the plants to the tiles, and also provide a certain amount of the right kind of fertiliser to get the plants to grow strongly. The only

29

real problem Richard has encountered is the fact that birds, presumably looking for resident insects, tend to peck at the growing mass in the winter. However, they leave them alone in the summer so recovery is pretty swift.

Of course there is a 'cheat's' method. Pre-planted sedum matting can be bought by the yard or even less from various companies, to create anything from the kind of pretty patch on a tiled roof that you are after to a whole green eco-friendly roof. Enviromat is just one company that does this, and also gives a lot of helpful advice on installation and maintenance.

SPOTTY HEBE

My mother has a problem with just one of a group of hebes grown close together in her garden near the East Sussex coast. The hebe in question developed black spots on the leaves, which then turned yellow and are now dropping off. What should she do to save the sickly member of the group and prevent the others from going the same way?
Tina, by email

It sounds as if this little shrub is suffering from a fungal leaf spot—similar to rose black spot. Your mother should try to clear up all the fallen leaves around the base of the plant so that spores don't linger in the soil, and she could also spray the shrubs with a systemic fungicide such as Systhane Fungus Fighter, which may go some way to control the disease. It is highly possible that this fungal disease will *not* spread to the other hebes since, in my experience, it only commonly takes hold of the varieties with larger leaves—and is most likely to do so when bushes are under stress from drought, overcrowding and so on. It may well be that this group of hebes has become too congested and needs thinning out or pruning. At the very least your mother should feed them all with a general fertiliser (such as blood, fish and bone) in the spring, and also mulch them with something moisture retaining and nourishing, such as well-rotted manure or home-made compost. If cosseted, the now-sickly plant will be better able to fight off the disease once the growing season gets well under way, when it can be trimmed back to make it less straggly and promote the production of new healthy shoots.

It is possible to get reasonable control of various leaf spots on shrubs—I have done it. But I am always aware that the diseases will very likely return if the plants in question are not consistently well cared for.

PRUNING SPRING-FLOWERING SHRUBS

By now, everyone's winter jasmine has dropped its last and the forsythia is probably in shabby tatters, so this might be a good time to get to grips with the basic principles that govern the pruning of these and other spring-flowering shrubs.

Shrubs that flower in 'spring' (that is, those that

start to flower at any time between January and mid-summer) do so mainly on growth that they made the previous year. We tend to cram shrubs into our gardens with a fairly clear idea in our mind's eye of how much space they are going to be allowed to occupy. Once they fill their allotted space they must be pruned, or they start to crowd each other and deteriorate, flowering only on the outermost, newest branches, while the older branches get increasingly woody and congested. As likely as not, someone gets the bit between their teeth and decides to 'tidy things up', frequently at one of the classic 'tidying' times of year, early spring or autumn. In the wrong hands, spring-flowering shrubs can thus have all their potential flowering shoots removed and be reduced to non-flowering leafy lollipops—or worse.

The best way to make sure you get the most out of your spring-flowering shrubs is to prune them the moment they have finished flowering, before they put out new growth from their shoot tips that will confuse the issue. There is no single specific time to prune early flowering shrubs. If you grow some of the most common that flower in succession—winter jasmine, forsythia, ceanothus, weigela and philadelphus—you will have pruning to do at regular intervals from March to July.

Pruning should be done by removing the shoots that have faded flowers on them, cutting back to where you can see fresh new growth starting to emerge lower down in the bush, or at least some good healthy buds. At the same time, to encourage the shrub to renew its woody undercarriage, it is a good idea to take out one or two older shoots from ground level. However, this depends very much on the growth habit of individual shrubs.

When the job is finished the shrub will look smaller, but still quite shapely and leafy. A feed with a general fertiliser will kick-start more growth, which will then carry flowers the following year. If you have got it right, the shrub should only need perhaps the merest smidgeon of re-shaping in the autumn—and absolutely no major surgery.

Of course, there are variations and exceptions. For example, most evergreen ceanothus varieties, which tend to have a short lifespan anyway, will not take kindly to vicious pruning of any kind and need a gentle touch each year. And all those rather slow-growing little evergreen spring smellies we love—*Daphne odora*, the skimmias, sarcococca and co—need only to have a few inches cut off their outer growth each year. 'Pruning' these may involve little more than picking small posies and bringing them into the warmth of the house where they release their scent more readily. This goes for lilac, too. Sparkly spring sun slanting through an open casement window on to a polished wooden table and a china jug of scented lilac has been a little domestic fantasy of mine for years. At least it turns out to be a horticulturally correct one.

INTRUDER IN THE GRASS

I am not normally fussy about my rather rough and ready lawn, but there is something that turns up in the grass at this time of year that I find infuriating. It looks superficially like grass, but has brown bristly flowers. I reluctantly tried

a lawn weedkiller last year, with little success.
Have you any suggestions?
Jay, by email

This nasty little weed is called field woodrush or *Luzula campestris*, and is one with which I am all too familiar. It can threaten to take over from grass on poorly nourished, damp, acid lawns, and is extremely hard to control.

If it is dry enough to mow—and it should be by now—then mow your lawn as often as you can while the woodrush is in flower, with the blade set at a height just sufficient to nip off those annoying bristles. This will help to control its spread, although it has creeping roots as well, so don't expect miracles. Since woodrush has narrow, grass-like leaves, it is hard to eradicate with just a single application of lawn weedkiller, so if you are really determined you will have to work a bit harder and apply a second dose later in the growing season. You could also feed your lawn to strengthen the lawn grasses, spike it to improve the drainage, and apply lime to the soil in the form of ground chalk next winter. I expect all this sounds as though I am recommending that you become 'fussy' about your lawn.

Actually I am not. The pragmatist in me recommends that, apart from a little more vim and vigour where your spring mowing is concerned, you learn to live with this weed. Woodrush flowers for only a few weeks, after which it is more or less absorbed into the messy tapestry that so many of us have to accept as a substitute for a fine greensward. Apply such energy as you have to the eradication of close-knit huddles of easy-to-winkle-out plantains, or gaudy dandelions that you can shrivel up with a quick spritz with a lawn spot weeder. In my view, these are the real beasties.

FOOD FOR THOUGHT

A reader from Loughborough who prefers to remain nameless admits rather sheepishly to never having fed the plants in her small garden. Everything seems to grow well enough, she says, and there are few casualties. She spreads the contents of her rather haphazard compost bin around her two rose bushes from time to time, but that is all. She asks if she should be doing more, if so what and why, and will it really make a difference? I must say I am not quite sure where to start with this, or how far I can go—bearing in mind that I am a gardener, not a soil scientist.

However 'natural', a garden is a highly artificial environment. In the wild, plants tend to feed themselves, their own foliage rotting down around them and being drawn into the soil where it will eventually do some good. Wild hedgerows collapse in winter and spring up again, fresh and fluffy every year, while traditionally grazed meadows are 'fed' by manure produced by the grazers. This goes on all around us very nicely without our help. But crammed together in gardens or allotments, plants are expected to flower, crop and generally over-perform for us while we scurry around mowing, cutting things down, clearing up autumn leaves and tidying away every scrap of undesirable old foliage. Soil can run out of oomph, eventually becoming sour and less fertile as nutrients drain away.

Home composting undoubtedly goes some way to undo the harm we do by being so 'tidy', and many gardeners do simply add composts and manures to their soil to improve its texture and feed their plants—and leave it at that. But few of us generate enough home-made compost for this to be sufficient, nor do we have easy access to enough good rotted manure. You can, if you get really carried away by the whole idea, find out what your soil needs by doing extensive soil fertility tests, although most gardeners I know don't bother, and simply add as much compost and other organic matter as they can muster, digging it in or applying it as a mulch, and back this up by casting about what is known as a 'balanced' fertiliser (see February, page 293) to beds and borders each year in spring, and maybe again in mid-summer.

Does all this nurturing make a difference? Those of us who do it certainly believe it does.

TURF AROUND YOUNG TREES

To make our life easier, we have recently turfed an area of the garden that contains fruit bushes and young fruit trees. My wife has read that you need to leave about a yard of clear ground around each fruit tree or they will not thrive, but I find that elsewhere in the garden where we have done this, the bare soil gets invaded by weeds—making even more work.

What is the best course of action?
Peter, by email

Young saplings growing in the wild struggle through all sorts of tangly grass and undergrowth, but as a consequence grow quite slowly. We expect rather more from things we put in our gardens, particularly fruit trees and bushes, and certainly they will do better in their early years if they do not have to compete with grass and weeds for water and nutrients. It makes sense, therefore, to keep an area approximately the same size as their branch span clear of other plants and I would be inclined to cut away completely the new turf from under the bases of your bushes and trees before it starts growing this season. The last thing you want to do is use a strimmer around young woody plants—you can easily damage their bark and kill them. Without the grass you will find it much easier to feed your plants annually, and also to mow.

If grass seedlings and weeds start to germinate, you could always knobble them with a product such as Weedol, which will 'burn' off young green growth without damaging woody stems (it is inactivated on contact with soil and doesn't leave harmful residues). Alternatively, you could keep the weeds permanently at bay by pegging down circular pieces of porous weed-smothering material—or even bits of upside-down old carpet—around each tree and covering it with a layer of composted or chipped bark.

WHAT TO DO WITH LEFTOVERS

I know for certain that emailer Brian is not the only gardener to kick himself for leaving garden chemical mixtures around in unlabelled, anonymous spray bottles. He killed a load of carefully nurtured seedlings by giving them a swish from something in a spray bottle that was close to hand—that turned out to be glyphosate weedkiller. He asked me to warn other gardeners.

The nanny in me compels me to add the following: we should never, ever, leave any garden chemicals around mixed up in unmarked cans and bottles. Any leftovers should immediately be poured away on waste ground (or a gravel drive, perhaps), but not down the drain. Bottles and containers should then be thoroughly rinsed out. Quite apart from the danger factor, most garden chemicals deteriorate rapidly once mixed up. Scared of Brian-style slip-ups, I tend to use red-topped pump bottles and red watering cans when using anything remotely nasty. Ready-mixed versions of many pesticides, fungicides and weedkillers are now sold in spray bottles, and this is clearly a sensible option for those who use them rarely and in small quantities. The formulations of these are always slightly different, in order to give them a helpfully long shelf life. We may hate paying the considerable extra for a small amount of a product in an annoying pistol-action bottle, and for the privilege of having no fiddly mixing to do, but for those who possess small gardens and/or short memories, it may be money well spent, and could mean the difference between plant life and death—as poor Brian now knows.

SLUGGING IT OUT

Did you know that in just a square yard of garden there are up to 50 slugs and snails? What, only 50, do I hear you say? What we all do know is that these ghastly things are truly the gardener's most hated foe. And although we think of them as a single problem, joined, as it were, at the hip, slugs and snails have very different lifestyles (apart from the obvious carrying-the-home-on-the back thing), different spheres of operation and even different dietary habits.

I won't honour the numerous species of slugs with their Latin names. It is the tiny ones you seldom see that do most of the damage—dark grey and black, they lurk under the soil surface and can demolish emerging spring shoots overnight, while their slightly larger beige cousins hang out in damp spring grass to decimate the flowers of early bulbs and later move on to spoil your spuds. Surprisingly perhaps, the slinky black and orange horrors, inches long, that you find oozing across the terrace at night actually do less damage. They all hide away when it is very cold or very dry, but mild moist weather, even in winter, has them all up and at it and on the scrounge. Worst of all, slugs are hermaphrodites, so they don't even need a mate— they all lay eggs and breed all the year round. Clusters of eggs, palely pearlescent in the dark, damp soil, turned up with a hoe, are viewed as caviar by birds (my hens snapped them up), hedgehogs, frogs and toads.

Smoothly lumbering, slightly fascinating snails are not just slugs with shells. They conveniently hibernate from late October and through the winter, breeding in late spring. They also shut up shop and hide in dry summer weather: crusty little gangs to be found, in my experience, in piles of old flower pots behind the shed, or tucked snugly up into ivy-covered walls. Protected by their shells from predators and drying winds, they can climb significant heights, bivouacking by day in places we seldom think of looking. Rounded up before the breeding season and released elsewhere, with any luck they make a banquet for song thrushes. The damage they do is huge and obvious. Wouldn't it be lovely if there was a fail-safe, kill/cure-all way of dealing with them? But this is a war that has to be fought on many fronts. Persistence is all, and there is now a huge array of stuff to help us.

Pellets: In addition to traditional slug pellets, there are now rainproof wildlife-friendly slug pellets containing ferric phosphate, for example Growing Success's Advanced Slug Killer. Once ingested, the slugs cease to feed and crawl away to die, generally underground, so there are no corpses to deal with. Or try 'feeding' snails with bran—it gives them terminal bellyache.

Dog-eat-dog biological control: A programme of Nemaslug—'re-constituted' nematodes that you water into soil—is pretty effective against slugs if used according to instructions, but is no use until the soil warms up, which makes it too late for protecting precocious border plants, but great for pre-treatment of the soil in veg beds. It does not clobber snails.

Nocturnal hunting: Snails can be hunted down either when in snooze-mode, as mentioned above, or on warm damp evenings when they are up to no good—torch and receptacle of salt water in hand. Don't fling them next door… they just come back.

Beer traps: Saucers of beer work just as well as purpose-made traps. Slugs and snails imbibe, drop in dead drunk and die. Traps need daily attention or they start to stink—and I get fed up with the whole palaver after a few weeks. Too often, ground beetles and other useful garden friends seem to find their way into traps, which is bad news.

Physical barriers: This is where things get interesting, I think. There are certain materials that slugs and snails won't cross and manufacturers, picking up on this, are constantly giving us new products. Both beasts particularly hate rough and abrasive surfaces that upset their slime-based movement, and copper (which gives them mild electric shocks), so you can surround and/or cover particularly vulnerable plants or even pots and raised beds with barriers that will basically stop them in their tracks. Vital points to remember when using barriers are: to treat the soil within them (with either nematodes or slug pellets) to ensure that you don't trap any nasties inside, for obvious reasons. And as the season gets under way, you have to ensure that leaves of protected plants don't touch those of neighbouring unprotected ones, or even walls and fences. Snails, as I have said, are determined climbers and, it would seem, abseilers.

I've had success with Slug Buggers, a lovely-sounding mixture of sheep's wool and sheep's poo extruded into pellet form that, once in contact with damp soil, forms a kind of hairy, nutrient-rich mat over and around plants, over which slugs will not

41

slither.

Especially rough grit, as sold by EcoCharlie, is working well too. A 3in (8cm) wide band of this is protecting the pretty sluglicious leaves of my *Brunnera macrophylla* 'Jack Frost' as I write. Several readers have written to say that coffee grounds (acquired in bulk from high-street coffee-shop chains) are effective too. All these barriers may need to be checked and topped up.

And then there is copper. Green Gardener's copper rings and bands (strips that you slot together yourself) are really effective. Copper sticky tape (the anti-snail version with a jagged edge) works best around pots and home-made barriers made of lawn edging, and stays in place for a couple of years, dulling down with age. Pots can be placed on Slug Shocka copper-impregnated fabric, or stood on ingenious copper-coated pot feet (all from Green Gardener). You can use Slug Shocka like a permeable membrane on the soil, too, and plant through it, while Doff's Socusil slug-repellent spray contains copper silicate solution.

Copperbed is a really exciting idea, I think—an epoxy resin paint to which you add powdered copper and apply in a wide strip, using the roller provided, to clean, dry wood, terracotta and other surfaces. This provides a brilliant, extremely long-lasting (10-year) solution, particularly for those building new smart raised beds.

Also working with the electric shock deterrent idea, there is even a build your own mini-electric fence system for protecting anything from individual pots and trees to large areas, from SnailAway.

(For a list of slug-resistant plants, see October, page 189.)

EGGSTRATERRESTRIALS?

While re-potting my standard fuchsias, which have been over-wintering in the greenhouse, I noticed some small orange eggs (2–3mm— about ⅛ in—diameter), and also some white grubs, about twice that size, which curled up when disturbed. Some of the fuchsia plants had very little root, so I assume the grubs had been eating them. I have removed as many eggs and grubs as I can see but I am sure some remain. What steps should I take now?
Bryan, Sutton Coldfield

Your greenhouse has clearly become a vine weevil (VW) playground. But the good news is that the orange 'eggs' are not in fact VW eggs at all—which I am told are smaller, soil coloured and thus undetectable. They are almost certainly granules of slow-release fertiliser, which must have been added to the compost of the plants you acquired most recently from nurseries. You are not the first person to assume they were VW eggs, I can assure you.

The bad news is that you have a real battle on your hands in the future, since adult weevils may be lurking somewhere in the greenhouse—they are past masters at this— and will undoubtedly strike again this year. I would have a spring clean if I were you, and stamp firmly on any adults—black, slow-moving, snouty beetles about ½in (1cm) long—that you discover. There may also be eggs in other potted plants, or in sheltered parts of the garden around favoured plants (heucheras, primulas, pansies).

There are two paths you can go down, one chemical, the other 'natural'. If you chose to use chemical control, you could re-pot those plants that seem to have enough roots left to survive, using a Levington compost that contains the insecticide imidacloprid, or use your normal compost and then drench it with Provado Vine Weevil Killer, which contains the same chemical. If you prefer not to use chemicals, then tap the soil off the remaining plants to remove any grubs. Robins adore them, so throw any grubs that you find on the lawn—or just empty the compost on to a plastic sheet and let the birds have a free-for-all. Later in the month, when the soil is warmer (above 5°C/41°F), you could water the pots with a solution containing VW-destroying nematodes: Nemasys Vine Weevil Killer is now widely available, in case any grubs or invisible eggs got past you, and also treat any suspect sites in the garden. You should have another go in autumn, or sooner if you see any adult VWs snooping around, or see the tell-tale 'notching' of leaf margins on lower branches of evergreens on which they feed. A layer of sand or gravel on top of potted plants may deter weevils from laying eggs.

Slip up just once and call them wine veevils by mistake and you are sunk for ever…

DAFFODIL MAYHEM

Jackie from Marlborough wonders what she should do about the ill-fated daffodils she has planted in the grass in her new garden. She is (probably wisely) digging out clumps of stumps— those that her husband mowed over earlier this spring. She would rather do this than have them suffer the same fate next year when, if they miraculously avoid being mowed again, they would undoubtedly come up 'blind' after this year's untimely savagery. She wonders about the survivors, those that escaped the mower and have managed to flower. Can she move them out of his way now, or should she hide the key for the mower while they die down naturally, before digging them up and storing them?

Mowing around isolated clumps of daffodils in grass is intensely frustrating, and the temptation to just mow straight over those that are 'in the way' is almost irresistible. So I think the answer here, before deciding what to do with which daffodils, is to call a truce with the husband, and agree to designate one area of the grass that will forever be an Absolutely No-Mow area until around the end of May, at least. This would give an opportunity to plant other things in the grass that will flower in spring. Snowdrops, camassias (like giant, upright bluebells) and fritillaries and maybe some delicate tulips would look wonderful, as would a touch of cow parsley, even.

As for those daffs, Jackie can, if she must, move them 'in the green' (i.e. before the leaves die down) to a safer site. They should then be watered and foliar fed with a liquid fertiliser such as Phostrogen a couple of times in the coming weeks. They will put on some sort of show next year, and be back to normal the year after. Or she can wait until the leaves go orange (about five weeks after flowering), then dig the bulbs up and store them somewhere cool and dry before replanting them in September. Bulbous plants need their leaves to remain intact after flowering to act as 'solar panels' to enable them to make the buds for the following year's flowers.

May

BORDER CORSETRY

Around this time, before gardens are properly decked out in floral finery, it is a real eye-opener to visit a smart, high-maintenance garden. There you will discover borders full of attractive, ingeniously woven hazel and willow plant supports, forests of twiggy 'pea-sticks' encircling crowds of juicy infant herbaceous shoots and roses tied with minute precision on to tailor-made supports that are veritable works of art. In high summer you see none of it, but this soon-to-be-invisible corsetry is an essential part of the classic stylised 'cottage' garden, and without it—or at least something similar—our herbaceous clumps can loll and flop all over the shop.

Some of my bigger border plants are simply supported every year by twigs of hazel and birch stuck into the ground around them. But I felt it was time I made more of an effort to join the grown-ups. It has been a case of going back to the drawing board—or rather the mail-order catalogue and garden centre—to replace and augment the bent and rusty plastic-coated wire hoops that have stood me in good stead since the 1980s.

I am gradually building up a supply of handsome rusted iron stakes with balls on the top that look good all the year round. Woven unobtrusively with a cat's cradle of jute twine, a group of these are great for supporting a tall clump. I also use them singly, attaching a length of twine and threading it through and around stems in a single plant clump for 'invisible' support. In addition to their mellow looks and infinite life, these iron stakes don't buckle and bend, so in my view they are well worth the investment.

Lower-growing plants benefit from support of other kinds. Many of my herbaceous geraniums, for example, look a thousand times better if they grow up through metal grids on legs in various sizes, which also provide discreet support for heavy-headed paeonies and oriental poppies. But I find that other stout, leafy plants may only need to be propped up by semi-circular hoops on two legs, the biggest versions of which, placed back to back, form rigid circlets for border giants.

No single gadget or method does the trick for all plants. Get to know your plants and what works best for them, and at what heights supports should be set. And put them in place sooner rather than later—early May is ideal—so that the plants can grow through and into them naturally. If you miss the boat, you can do an awful lot of damage wading through thigh-high foliage and flowers to shore things up.

EAVESDROPPING

I listen in every year at Chelsea... I heard one woman state categorically that there were 'too many flowers' in one garden, while another complained that she didn't like 'all that dead grass' (a fashionable brown carex, presumably). Elsewhere, a group was clearly bemused at the lack of floral profusion in an Australian garden (which was admittedly dominated by svelte,

48

curvaceous decking). One explained to the others: 'Well it's barren, like Australia, innit.'

PESTS OF THE SEASON

Capsid bugs

Lucy, a Londoner, has been painstakingly investigating a source of great irritation in her garden, namely the cause of the hideously puckered shoot tips and failure to flower of a large assortment of plants. She lists choisyas, fuchsias and crocosmia among the worst affected, and has identified the culprit as capsids—leggy little bugs that proved extraordinarily elusive until she worked out where they like to hang out (on the underside of leaves), and that they move like greased lightening if they detect even as much as a potential predator's shadow. What, she asks, will defeat these horrid things?

As usual, getting to grips with the life cycle of garden pests enables you to work out a plan of campaign to defeat them. Capsid bugs, about a quarter of the size of a little fingernail, are pretty unremarkable. They can overwinter in nearby hedges and trees (particularly apple and hawthorn), migrating in spring to all manner of favoured plants, laying eggs in young shoot tips. The tiny unseen grubs of this first generation feast within the growing buds, totally destroying developing flowers. The damage they do only manifests itself weeks later, as leaves emerge from buds puckered, their centres peppered with tiny holes and with a shocking lack of—or badly distorted—flower buds. By this time the grubs will have literally gone to ground, where they pupate

49

and, if weather conditions suit, a second generation of adult capsids will emerge to have another go—laying eggs on any shoots or leaves that take their fancy. In my own garden the second flush of flowers of my generally prolific 'Bonica' rose have been badly affected, along with the evergreen foliage of my formerly gorgeous purple sage.

So what can be done for next year? Lucy managed, through her persistence, to catch and squash numerous of the little beasts on her crocosmia, but I would imagine that this was just the tip of the iceberg. Regrettably, I can see no other way of dealing with this garden horror story without resorting to chemical control. The best approach is to try to stop the antics of the first generation by spraying plants known to be attractive to them with Provado Ultimate Bug Killer, which contains thiacloprid, a systemic insecticide. Spray plants just as their buds start to develop, in late April—repeating the procedure a few weeks later, just after mid-summer. In the case of really serious infestation, gardeners with apple or hawthorn trees could give them a winter wash to try to knobble the overwintering adults (look for Growing Success's organic product based on plant oils, available at garden centres).

Solomon's seal sawfly
William emailed me asking about the small caterpillars that attack his Solomon's seal plants (*Polygonatum odoratum*) each summer and reduce them to skeletons. What are they, and what can he do about them?

The caterpillars are the larvae of the Solomon's

seal sawfly. They overwinter in cocoons in the soil and the adult flies emerge in May and June—and this is the time to deal with them. The females lay eggs in the leaf stalks, which hatch out within days. The larvae feed in busy little groups for the following month, usually on the undersides of the leaves so that the damage is done almost before you notice what is going on. They then go back into the soil, remaining as cocoons for the winter and the whole thing starts all over again—unless they are stopped. The only good thing to be said for the Solomon's seal sawfly is that there is only one generation produced per season, so it is possible to catch them at it and spray with an insecticide or pick them off laboriously by hand—once you know when and where to look for them.

Mullein moths and shield bugs

The leaves of Jane in Kent's biennial yellow verbascums were reduced to tatters last summer by the handsome black and yellow striped caterpillars of the mullein moth. This year her plants have been invaded by something different: large, greenish flat-backed beetles that are having a 'fair old time' amid the foliage, she says. She dealt with the caterpillars with a single, carefully timed spray of a systemic insecticide (I use Provado Ultimate Bug Killer a couple of weeks before my verbascums flower, and before the moths 'strike'), and wonders if she should spray these alien-looking beetles too?

Jane's new perceived enemy are commonly known as shield beetles, more correctly called shield bugs. Bugs and beetles are not the same thing at all, as I was once sternly informed by a reader. Bugs have piercing mouthparts, beetles have biting ones, as I understand. And while these shield bugs do pierce leaves to suck sap, they do relatively little visible damage to the verbascums on which they like to, as it were, make hay. They should not be regarded as a major pest, large and slightly menacing-looking though they may seem.

BULB MARKERS

I was taken to task recently by a visitor who suggested that the assortment of (admittedly ancient and leaning) bamboo canes that I had put in my newly laid-out formal herbaceous border to remind me where I had planted my tulips was rather 'letting the side down'. How does anyone avoid putting a trowel through his or her bulbs without doing something similar?
Janet, *by email*

If you can't stand looking at winter borders decorated with purpose-made plant labels (which do annoyingly tend to get mysteriously shifted about), you have to devise a system that suits you. If your bamboo canes do the trick and really don't offend you, then don't take any notice of what anyone else says.

Plagued increasingly as I am by OPA (Obsessive Planter's Amnesia), the life expectancy of bulbs in my own garden was considerably enhanced when I eventually abandoned proper labels and started using wooden kebab sticks (the sort sold in packets in supermarkets) to mark where I had planted them. (I do keep a note indoors of varieties planted, but then can't remember where I put it…) Kebab sticks are discreet enough not to attract the attention of anyone except those actually working close to the soil (me); they are long enough to stick well into the ground so that squirrels, cats, etc can't shift them; yet short enough not to poke you in the eye. Their bright newness dulls down nicely within a few weeks and they last just long enough—at least a season—before they rot away. You can use them to mark the position of each member of a group of lilies (even in pots) and subsequently replace them very carefully with proper supporting canes as the lilies show their heads later in the spring. Or you can use them to mark the position of a random scattering of bulbs in a border, making a point of always putting a stick to the north, south, east and west of the group, for example. You should give them a whirl.

Alternatively, if you go for that sort of thing, you can buy jaunty little metal markers in the shape of flowers (look for them in those wildly extravagant garden-gizmo shops that are such fun to browse in).

AND MARKER PENS…

On a related subject, Ginny from Henley-on-Thames despairs of ever finding a really permanent marker pen for her plant labels. Personally, I find that when needs must, a silver marker pen on black plastic labels is easy to read, lasts indefinitely and looks low-key and classy—certainly a lot better than those horrid plastic flags that nurseries latch on to so many plants.

Silver pen lasts well on slate labels too—and it's cheaper to make labels from broken slates from a builders' merchant than it is to buy them readymade, according to emailer Clare.

TULIP AFTERCARE

Mel does not want to go to the trouble of lifting her border tulips and storing them, but she wants to ensure they flower next year. What should she do?

There is no guarantee tulips will survive and prosper from year to year—some just don't like our winter wet and they all seem to object to heavy clay soil. To give them their best chance I cut down the flower heads and stalks the moment their petals fall to just above the second leaf, which makes them less messily obtrusive while leaving enough leaf to give the tulip energy to make the following year's bud. I then foliar feed them and let them die down naturally, making sure there are markers in the soil (see above) so I know where they are before I eventually remove the yellowed remains of their leaves. You quickly find out which tulips are tough survivors. 'White Triumphator' is a goodie, as is 'Orange Emperor'. In fact the lily-flowered ones all seem to do well in my own heavy clay.

For those of you who *do* want to go to the trouble of lifting tulips, to be on the safe side, you should let your tulip leaves go yellow and start to die off before you lift the bulbs. The leaves should be cut or gently pulled away from the bulbs, the soil should be carefully brushed off them and any that are damaged should be discarded. Once cleaned, they should be dried overnight on a tray and then dusted with a fungicide before being stored away in paper bags until you are ready to plant them again next November. Do not, as I have done in the past, fail to write a description of the flower—and the location that they were grown in—clearly on the bag. Just the name of the variety is, if you think about it, not all that helpful.

SPANGLISH BLUEBELLS

We have recently moved house and have found that there is a large patch of very vigorous bluebells in one corner of our shady lawn. I suspect that they are Spanish bluebells, but I am not sure. How can I tell the difference? And if I decide they are Spanish, what should I do about them?
M P, Battersea, London

It is really not hard to tell a Spanish bluebell (*Hyacinthoides hispanica*) from a pure native English one (*H. non-scripta*). Spanish bluebells are altogether stouter, taller, with wider leaves and more upright stems, and paler blue flowers that, unlike English bluebells, have no scent. The altogether finer, slightly darker stems of true English bluebells carry flowers on one side only, and curve as they age.

For some time there has been a pretty strong campaign to get rid of more robust Spanish bluebells because there is apparently evidence that they are slowly starting to knock out our native plants and that hybrids are gradually invading our precious woodlands. In truth, most garden bluebells are hybrids anyway. If you lived in the country, and especially if you lived in a bluebell woods area, it would be worth trying to clear out any obvious 'aliens', and certainly deadhead them to slow down their spread. However, getting rid of bluebells is not easy. Digging them out is well nigh impossible and you will inevitably leave behind bits and pieces of bulbs that will come back year after year, as well as stir up dormant seed in the soil. Some determined gardeners go to great lengths, crushing leaves underfoot and repeatedly using a glyphosate weedkiller on them, digging out bulbs and practically mangling them before disposing of them.

Personally, I feel it is up to you how far you take things. Yours is an urban garden and your bluebells are very likely to be hybrids— only 'Spanish-ish'. You can spend a lot of time and energy turning your garden upside down in an attempt to get rid of them, doing your bit for conservation—but what will you really achieve? Who is to say that a few feet away on the other side of the fence your unwitting neighbours are not delighted at, and encouraging the proliferation of, more of the same?

WHAT TO DO WITH HEBES

Should you trim off the dead heads of hebes in the autumn or spring, or just leave them alone?
David, Orpington, Kent

Being neat, evergreen and flowery, hebes make useful 'punctuation mark' plants for small gardens and need little maintenance for their first few years, other than a bit of deadheading in late spring (to answer your question). After a few years of doing this, however, hebes can get too big for their boots. At which point it is all too easy to go 'eek, what now?' and proceed to get it all wrong, cutting back hard into old wood too early in the year and risking losing them completely. The fact that these evergreen flowering shrubs come from rather milder New Zealand means that many of them need sensitive pruning. As a general rule it is wise to regard them as slightly tender, and only prune them every second or third year, in late spring or early summer, after which you should not expect them to return to their former neat selves for several months. A way of lessening the shock to the system might be to cut back about a third of the branches around now, so that the shrub is encouraged to start to make new growth under the protective cover of the remainder of its canopy. In June, perhaps (depending on how warm your garden is), you could then cut back the rest of the framework of branches, and the new growth will fill out quite quickly.

GROUND ELDER AND GLYPHOSATE

I have tried to get rid of a patch of ground elder growing between and under a group of rhododendrons by digging out its roots, but the soil is very compacted and the shoots and leaves just break away in my hands. I decided to spray the patch with a glyphosate weedkiller. The leaves that I sprayed became mottled, but the clump then produced more leaves that looked, if anything more vigorous than ever. Where have I gone wrong?
Roger, by email

I think you used the weedkiller too early in the growing season. Although its first shoots appear in April, ground elder doesn't really get into full swing until late May, so early treatment is, frustratingly, unlikely to be very effective.

Glyphosate weedkillers (such as Roundup and Tumbleweed) work by being absorbed through the leaves of plants. The chemical travels downwards to the roots, which, after about two weeks, start to die off. With a well-established patch of ground elder the first leaves that appear are merely the tip of the iceberg and to kill the extensive invasive root system of this plant you need to wait until there is the largest possible amount of leaf showing. You should now let more new leaves develop and wait before you apply the spray again—around the middle or end of June. Once the leaves start to pucker and wilt, you could then cover the patch with a sheet of

58

black plastic (covered, for aesthetic reasons if necessary, with a layer of composted bark) and leave it in place until the autumn. This should see the ground elder off, but any that survives will be easy to dispatch next spring.

One further tip: water the ground elder thoroughly the night before you do the business with the weedkiller. This will plump it up and make it more susceptible, I am told.

MULCH MOWERS

I would appreciate some advice about mowers that mulch the grass they have just cut.
James, by email

Some gardeners find using a mulch-mower the ultimate gardening liberation—and I can kind of see why. The mowers save time and effort by disposing of the just-cut grass for you instead of collecting it in a box, so all that laborious emptying and tiresome management of smelly grass heaps becomes a thing of the past. They work by chopping up the grass extremely finely and throwing it back downwards into the turf. I have not been tempted by one of these mowers so I have no personal experience on which to draw, but I understand that the system works well on short grass that is cut regularly when it is relatively dry. The chopped-up grass acts as a constant nitrogen-rich grass feed, apparently, when the system works well. However, I have friends who say it is less than ideal for long, damp grass, and results in a lot of 'chopped spinach'. These great wads of residue get walked into the house on the bottom of boots and paws—a small, practical, but very important domestic detail when there are children and dogs concerned.

WILD GARLIC

Patricia from St Albans has had a lucky escape. She should be very thankful that the wild garlic given to her last year by a Cornish groundsman because she was 'very taken with it growing everywhere' failed to survive. It is a pernicious, virtually uncontrollable weed and is best just admired in the wild, as many other readers battling with it will no doubt testify. For those afflicted: glyphosate followed by a covering of thick black plastic might just about see it off. Digging merely disperses it, I am told.

DANDELION THUMB

My neighbours have a very lax attitude to the dandelions that live in the grass bordering their drive, and as a result my own rather neglected grass has gradually been invaded by them. I would prefer not to treat my lawn with weedkiller. Is there a knack to just controlling the dandelions by digging them out?
Bob, Norwich

The problem with digging out dandelions, as you have no doubt discovered, is that their long, juicy taproot invariably snaps, and as a consequence the plants re-grow within a few

60

days or weeks, often with double heads and therefore the potential to bloom twice as strongly. This is the time of year when gardeners with less than perfect lawns develop a dandelion thumb—permanently stained from the sap of hastily removed dandelion heads—since new ones seem to duck under the mower and open every time our backs are turned.

If you tackle your dandelions when they are mere dandecubs, you will obviously have more success at digging them out in one piece. There are various tools designed to help—I have a particularly good long skinny dandelion trowel by Sneeboer that is sharp on three sides—but an old pointed kitchen knife with a long blade is quite handy. Dig down vertically all around the rosette of leaves before you even think of giving the whole plant a little tug. An alternative would be to go around depositing salt in the middle of each plant, or to use a tiny amount of weedkiller where it is needed via an aerosol spot weeder designed for use on lawns (Bayer makes one). Meanwhile, keep on removing flower heads from your lawn before they turn into more 'clocks', and hope and pray that the wind blows your neighbours' seeds in the opposite direction.

NETTLE BREW

I am often asked about making a fertiliser brew from nettles, so here is a 'recipe' I was given some years ago. You will need the following:

2lb (1kg) of nettles (or guess the amount—who on earth is actually going to weigh nettles?)
2 gallons (10 litres) of water
1 bucket with a tight lid
1 measuring jug
1 watering can
1 clothes peg (for your nose—the brew smells absolutely vile)

Leave to steep for three to four weeks. You should dilute one part of this foul brew in ten parts of water before using it, so that it looks like tea. Any that is left over at the end of the growing season should be poured, sludge and all, into your compost heap. Yuk.

TRACHELOSPERMUM IN TROUBLE

I have a problem with a previously happy and healthy **Trachelospermum jasminoides** *on my south-facing house wall. During the winter the leaves turned reddish. Now many of them are covered with a black soot. Although the soot does wipe off, cleaning the entire plant would be an impossible task. The plant still looks, despite the red leaves, fairly vigorous. What can I do about the soot?*
Anne, Whitley Bay, Tyne and Wear

Whenever I have banged on about this plant, describing its attributes—sensibly proportioned, evergreen, white jasmine-like flowers with a stunning scent—I may have failed to mention its two not uncommon problems. Firstly it dislikes long, bitterly cold winters, even when suitably placed against a warm house wall. In addition to nipping shoot tips, some or all of the normally shiny healthy leaves turn russet red and eventually drop, and plants are slow to get cracking and flower the following spring/summer. The other problem, the 'soot', is caused by a mould that grows on the excretions of tiny scale insects, similar to those that cause problems on the leaves of camellias and to which trachelospermum seems to be susceptible. It sounds as if your plant has a bad infestation. If you look on the mid-rib of the undersides of leaves you may see the perpetrators—they look like tiny beige flat discs, but they are quite hard to spot.

As you say, to 'wash' your plant would be a nightmare, but you could treat it with a systemic insecticide that also works by direct contact and try to wet the backs as well as the fronts of as many leaves as possible. Since trachelospermum is happiest in soil that is slightly acid, you could give it a restorative liquid feed that contains sequestered iron—such as Maxicrop.

PRUNING CAMELLIAS

We have lots of splendid camellias that are doing so well that they are beginning to take over the paths of our cottage garden. I fear for them somewhat, since my husband's greatest gardening joy is pruning. Before he sets to, please can you tell us—can camellias be pruned? If so, when and by how much?
Ann, Wigtownshire, Scotland

Somehow it has got into gardening lore that there are some shrubs you 'can't prune'. Camellias have gained themselves a reputation for being sensitive and untouchable and are thus tiptoed round by many a nervous gardener, but they can in fact be pruned. They are particularly slow-growing evergreens and are best planted where they can gradually expand without being fiddled with too much. But if they get out of hand—and they do—camellias are best pruned in late spring, just after they have flowered and are putting on a rapid growth spurt. Even with careful treatment they may well take several years to settle down and produce enough growth that will ripen and flower profusely for future decades.

So, once the plants have flowered, it's safe to let your husband cut them back. Suggest that he also feeds them with a fertiliser appropriate for acid-loving plants (Vitax make one for conifers and rhododendrons), but he should accept that the new growth produced will not flower for at least a year, maybe two. With that in mind, this is not the sort of job on which he can be let loose every year. So make sure you keep an eye on him.

A CHELSEA CHOPPER

Emailer Norman is keen to share his solution to over-vigorous sedums that flop. A year ago I advised him that he should split and replant them with none of the home comforts that other plants enjoy—no compost, general fertiliser, etc—on the grounds that sedums do well and stay more compact if grown on poor, dry soil. Norman's soil is already pretty ropey, he says, so having followed my advice, he thought sterner measures would be needed in the future. He took a tip from a French nurseryman who told him to cut his sedums down by half in the middle of the season, when they were about 1ft (30cm) high. This he duly did, and this year they have been standing to attention impeccably.

Much has been written about the 'Chelsea Chop'—the name given by those in the know to the practice of cutting plants down early in the season by varying degrees, or pinching out their growing tips, in order to manipulate both their height and their flowering time—kind of 'live heading', if you like—so that they look their best for the Chelsea flower show. I have been fiddling around along these lines in my own garden. An *Anthemis tinctoria* 'Sauce Hollandaise', planted in really rich soil in a brand new border, threatened to take over the world, outgrowing its support and sprawling alarmingly all over neighbouring, less gutsy plants. I chopped half of it back quite

65

roughly by about 2ft (60cm) in order to rescue its neighbours. As a result, just as the flowers from the undisciplined half of the plant faded, the other half came spectacularly into flower. *Verbena bonariensis,* growing in a rather exposed site and similarly chastened mid-season, flowered with twice the vigour but at half the height, and I gather that great things can be achieved by cutting the heads of phlox in July, before they flower. This is what I call gardening with knobs on. I utterly approve—I just have to find the time to do it…

Summer

June

MIND THE GAP

Not for me gardens planted with lines of lonely-looking soldiers standing to attention in a parade ground of prinked-over naked soil. I like gardens that are stuffed. I'm not even that fussed about the odd weed, about plants being 'unusual' or (heaven forbid) 'fashionable', as long as they are massed together to make a seamless tapestry—like June hedgerows before the local council flailing machines have reduced them to chopped spinach. Exuberant gardens are, I feel, a testament to the enthusiasm and obsessions of their owners and make me smile with pleasure. But they also inevitably have their dodgy moments, when unforeseen plant deaths, freak weather and misjudgement can render the tapestry temporarily threadbare in places at crucial moments.

My full garden early in the season is largely achieved with the use of various cottagey old faithfuls such as forget-me-nots and honesty. Each year I shake the seed heads of the former into the soil in my blue and white catmint-and-allium beds. Their froth of pale blue hides the soil between the emerging catmint and helps to disguise the ugly allium leaves as they fade. But I thin the seedlings out considerably each autumn, transplanting trowelfuls to borders where they perform the same function for tulips, but are pulled up before they drop their seed. Biennial white honesty is encouraged to form fairly unpredictably sized

69

colonies here and there. They look particularly good at the back of borders and spectacular under the cherry trees. The best plants are left *in situ* for their opaque papery skeletons, but seedlings need to be thinned out in their first season so that plants can mature to a decent size the following year. In order to keep the white colony 'pure', I restrict purple-flowered honesty to my gravel garden, where it looks luminous with tellimas and *Euphorbia polychroma*. Another handsome, tall, biennial early performer with dull greyish leaves and an acid yellow flower is *Isatis tinctoria*, a member of the brassica family that used to be used to make the dye woad. And, of course, my garden would be nothing without foxgloves. Any rogue seedlings are relocated when young, to create haphazard statement-making crowds here, there and everywhere.

So much for more or less natural, spring soil-covering fillers. Worrying gaps in a later summer border need a little more forethought, and I take cuttings of a few half-hardies to use in emergencies. My favourites are a pale daisy, *Argyranthemum* 'Jamaica Primrose', and *Senecio viravira*, a useful grey foliage plant with filigree leaves. These fast-growing shrubby plants will make a big statement in a single season, and will close up major gaps in borders in a matter of a few weeks. Tall annual white tobacco plants (*Nicotiana affinis*) are invaluable, and I also use those hanging-basket foliage standbys *Helichrysum petiolare*, both grey and lime green forms, which make wonderful clamberers/ sprawlers in sun and shade if planted in the ground and allowed to grow unchecked.

Finally, there is real stage management and manipulation. I have just whipped out a load of tulips (treating them strictly as annuals), and replaced them with my cannas, already with 2ft (60cm) high stripy shoots on them. These were dug up last autumn and kept in pots in my greenhouse. Also in the wings are heavy glazed pots (heavy so they don't topple, glazed so they keep in the moisture) of tall dahlias, mirabilis, acidanthera and scented lilies. These can stand around looking stylish in their own right or, if needs be, can be plopped into borders to fill up temporary spaces created when I cut back the first flush of flowering from regular border perennials. All that fiddly work to make a garden look like a hedgerow? Well, yes, I'm afraid so.

CONTROLLING AN ANTI-SOCIAL CLIMBER

Jo has emailed to say she has a so-called evergreen honeysuckle that is messy and straggly, and wants to know when she should prune it—bearing in mind the fact that she does not care too much about missing a year's flowering. Generally I say do it in March—because on the whole we are not sitting out in our gardens at that time of year and so are less likely to be offended by the appalling mess that radical cutting back of this untidy honeysuckle always creates. And anyway *Lonicera japonica* will cover its hideous woodiness with fresh greenery very quickly at this prime growing time of year. However, if Jo has the stomach for such ghastly work now, she could tackle it in the summer months—it will certainly not do it any harm. The honeysuckle, once re-grown, may

71

produce a few flowers as late as October this year—but won't really get into its stride until next year. By which time it will probably need pruning again. No prizes for guessing this is *not* my favourite honeysuckle; it's one I regard as totally unsuitable for garden fences and small gardens generally.

BOXING CLEVER

Sammy from Hampshire sent me a somewhat panic-stricken email about two box balls, originally about 18in (45cm) high and now rather shaggy, that she has not dared to clip yet. Her heart is in her mouth, she says. Are there any helpful and encouraging tips I can give her?

Of course, before engaging the brain and putting fingers to laptop, I had to go out and prune my own box balls to see if indeed there is a knack to it. Ten balls (and one blistered thumb) later, here are my thoughts.

Box pruning is best done in early June, and perhaps again (a lesser tidy-up job) in August. If cut later than this, subsequent autumn growth is vulnerable to frost—although you can smarten up the bushes when they are dormant in winter. I doubt if anyone looks forward to the job of clipping box with much enthusiasm, although I suspect that it is far less of a sleepless-night-causing job for those who have a natural eye for straight lines, symmetry and so on. Whether you have a good 'eye' or not, the job is inevitably tedious, involving a lot of bending and knee crunching.

For the big June cut, it helps if you get the

equipment right, choose a day that is not blisteringly hot, and make sure you will not have to hurry. Personally I find that kitchen scissors are easier to use than those trendy-looking sheep-shearing things that are sold for the purpose. I have also made myself a Box Bib—a 5ft (1.5m) square of fabric (in my case an old heavy-weight cotton-backed plastic tablecloth) with a slit cut in it and a hole in the centre—rather in the style of a hairdresser's cape. This gets placed around various subjects before they get the chop, to collect most of the bits.

Feeling comfortable clipping box has a lot to do with confidence, and the more you do it the easier it gets. I find that it is best to start at ground level, removing the lowest woody shoots from right underneath the balls, to give them that dumplings-barely-in-touch-with-the-ground look that is so fetching. Then I take off a swathe of new growth—it could be as much as about 3in (8cm) all around the base of the ball—which will act as a guide for the rest. On a 'mature' box ball, it will be clear how much to cut off: you will be removing practically all the new bright green soft growth. If you grow your own box balls and they are still developing, then you will need to be a little less severe and leave about 1in (2.5cm) of the new growth to build up the required density. The best box balls are grown quite slowly, which is why they are expensive to buy.

It would seem that our natural tendency is to take more off the top than the sides, so that over the years balls can tend to become rather squat and less than spherical. Starting with this swathe round the base, rather than starting from the top,

73

helps to counteract this, I find. It is really important to keep altering the position from which you are cutting, to stand right over the ball if space allows and to keep straightening up (and stretching your spine) to take a look at your work from all angles. Bash the ball gently from time to time so you can see how things are shaping up. The worst bit comes at the end, to my mind. Trying to get the 'bib' out from under without spilling the clippings all over the place is well nigh impossible. Hairdressers are not much good at this bit, either.

CLEMATIS PRUNING

Olive has a *Clematis cirrhosa* 'Wisley Cream' and Jennifer has a messy *Clematis* 'Miss Bateman'. Both of them are unsure when and how to cut them back, and since I suspect that there are others out there who are unsure about clematis pruning in general, here is one of my brief 'rough guides' which may be of some help.

The clematis tribe divides itself broadly into three groups: 1, 2 and 3. The first group is the earliest to flower and includes the *montanas*, evergreens *armandii* and *cirrhosa* and some of the newer prolific dwarf varieties such as *cartmanii* 'Avalanche'. If they have been planted where they are destined to get out of hand—as most are—they should be pruned immediately their flowers fade (and plucked-at again in July if they are really unruly). They all bloom on the shoots produced immediately after they finish flowering the previous year, so it almost goes without saying that you should not prune these when tidying up the garden in autumn or winter. This, then, should answer Olive's question.

Jennifer's clematis, however, belongs to slightly trickier group 2, which also flowers principally on the previous season's growth but slightly later, and then goes on to produce a few extra flowers in late summer. 'Miss Bateman', 'The President', 'Nelly Moser' and co should all be on their last flowering legs by now and should shortly be trimmed lightly, very lightly, so as not to spoil their late summer show. It is tempting to do no pruning at all to this often spectacular group (which also includes the less-showy *macropetala*), but failure to do so results, within a few years, in a nasty mass of twiggy stems, unsightly when not in flower and eventually making an increasingly weak show. A really catastrophic 'bird's nest' can be rescued by being cut down in early spring: the clematis will quickly produce a plethora of shoots, but of course these will be unlikely to produce any flowers until the following and subsequent years.

Group 3, the later summer-flowering clematis, are by far the easiest to prune. Because they produce all their flowers on the current season's growth, they can be cut down, to within 2ft (60cm) of the ground even, in October—or left until February or even March and reduced then.

INVISIBLE MENDING FOR LAWNS

I have been using a spot weeder on my lawn. I have had considerable success getting rid of the weeds, but am now left with numerous brown patches about 3–4in (8–10cm) across. What do I do next?
Tony, Kendal, Cumbria

However careful you are when targeting your lawn weeds with a spot weeder (see May, page 60), it seems that there is bound to be a certain amount of, shall we say, 'collateral damage'. The wide rosettes of the dandelion leaves, celandines or whatever it may be that you are trying to eradicate, will have killed the grass plants immediately adjacent anyway, so when the weed goes there is bound to be a brown patch of some sort. A technique I used years ago in my first garden, where I had more time to correct such irritations, has stood me in good stead recently since I have started to try to improve my dandelion-infested patch, and may be useful for you too. I trawl through the borders looking for the stray grass seedlings that are inevitably around, winkle them out with a fork, rough up the soil in the brown patches on my lawn and plant one or two in the middle of each, snipping them down a little with a pair of scissors to make them sprout. This may sound utterly laughable, I know, and no doubt will be dismissed by some as mere 'women's work', but I can assure you that the technique is spectacularly effective. The transplanted seedlings 'weeded' out of the borders establish really quickly and (unlike little patches of grass grown from fresh seed) are tough and don't show, while the existing lawn simply closes ranks around them. It really is invisible mending.

ON BEING BAMBOOZLED

I received a long email from an elderly couple in Devon, clearly distressed about an invasion of bamboo from a neighbour's garden. Some of the stems of this bamboo reach 20ft (6m), complained the writer, and shoots of it are starting to appear in raised beds in his garden in which he grows shrubs and vegetables. What can be done to control the creeping monster? He has no wish to fall out with his neighbour, he says.

In the first instance Mr P, as I will call him, can sever below ground level all the shoots that have appeared in isolation in his garden and remove whatever he can with a garden fork. He could then put down a physical vertical barrier on the boundary, using corrugated iron sheets or paving slabs—weed-smothering membrane or bits of pond liner are simply not strong enough. The barrier should stick up above soil level to stop shoots from arching over the top and should be around 18in (45cm) deep.

Weedkillers can be used on anything that pops up in Mr P's raised beds thereafter. Given the proximity of his other plants, Mr P will probably prefer to use a garden-friendly glyphosate weedkiller, in mid-summer, when the bamboo has got into full swing. Again, he should cut back the tallest shoots since he will be unable to reach them with a sprayer or watering can without risking damage to other plants. He should take care only to spray unwanted greenery and use plastic sheets or bin bags to protect shrubs and other plants, and only use a sprayer on a completely windless day. The plastic can be removed once the weedkiller is dry.

Not wanting to fall out with neighbours is all very well, but I do feel that before they do anything this couple should talk about the problem with them, since they may, behind their 20ft (6m) screen, be blissfully unaware of the distress their plant is causing. Co-operation between households would make the whole matter much easier.

I hope that this acts as a warning to others who are looking for quick screening and automatically think of bamboo. You need to do careful research: there are only a few varieties that will 'stay put'—the vast majority are, to a lesser or greater degree, fast-moving thugs. Somehow bamboo has become the ultimate modern plant. Probably the reasons are understandable: the quest for instant privacy in our increasingly small, increasingly 'lived-in' gardens, coupled with more exotic tastes fuelled by foreign travel. Planting a potentially invasive bamboo in a hole cut in weed-smothering membrane blanketed in gravel just makes the problem of controlling it more difficult, as many are now finding out. One solution, perhaps, if bamboo is a must, is to plant it in large containers, using it as an ultimately disposable temporary screen, while more manageable plants—evergreen, flowering shrubs, for example (of which there are plenty)—are allowed to grow up and establish behind or around them.

A BIG HAIRY FORGET-ME-NOT

More than one reader has written to me about a 'big hairy forget-me-not' that they can't get rid of. I presume this is alkanet, *Pentaglottis sempervirens*, a member of the *Boraginaceae* family (as are, not surprisingly, borage, forget-me-nots and anchusa). Alkanet, a madly self-seeding, coarse-leaved perennial, is almost universally loathed it would seem, except by me. I have to admit that in my various gardens I have always given alkanet limited permission to 'invade' usefully where absolutely nothing else will grow and flower—at the base of walls or rough hedges and on banks in deep shade, for example. Because of the almost season-long succession of deep blue borage-like flowers, I forgive its uncomfortable hairiness—although I don't let it go unchecked by any means.

The secret of controlling it is to wrench out the brittle, unpleasantly hairy flower stems (wearing gloves) as they age and before they go to seed (they will almost immediately produce new ones, making it one of the longest season flowerers of all), and to recognise and winkle out any rogue seedlings when they are in their infancy. The former just needs a bit of vigilance, the latter is more difficult until you get the measure of things. The seedlings could, to uninitiated optimists, look like much-coveted foxglove seedlings, although they get much bigger much more quickly. To ascertain which is which, if nothing else, one touch will tell you: young foxglove leaves are silky; alkanet is, from the word go, noticeably hairy.

As for total obliteration? You have to treat mature alkanet as you would any other thug plant. Digging is almost impossible because of the deep, brittle root. So there is nothing for it: glyphosate weedkiller, such as Roundup, best used when the plants are in full growth in mid-summer, and repeated before the end of the season if they dare show their faces again.

TEN SNIPPETS OF INFORMATION
ABOUT ROSES

Choosing and planting
1. If you want a long flowering season plus an old-fashioned-style flower, Hybrid Musk roses or English Roses are a good bet. All have some scent and a few (such as English Rose 'Gertrude Jekyll') smell glorious. Old shrub roses have immense glamour and are considered incredibly smart, but have a painfully short flowering season, so barely earn their keep in smaller gardens.
2. If you don't relish the general high maintenance of roses but love the smell, a hedge of disease-free, repeat-flowering, deliciously scented Rugosa roses is a convenient option—and will also produce colourful rose-hips the size of cherry tomatoes.
3. Whatever anyone else says, you *can* plant roses at the 'wrong' time (i.e. mid-summer, if needs be), if you do it by first sinking the whole caboodle—recently watered rose, pot and all—into carefully prepared moist soil, lifting it out to leave a perfect imprint of the pot. Then de-pot the rose swiftly, plop it into the resulting exactly right-sized hole, firm it gently, then mulch. I have done it repeatedly, so I know.

80

4. Using mycorrhizal fungi such as Rootgrow when planting bare-rooted roses (at the 'right' time, when they are dormant in winter) in my experience really does make for sturdier, healthier bushes. The fungi boost the plants' own roots and help them extract nutrients and water more efficiently (see also November, page 206).

Pruning and training
1. You are unlikely to kill a rose by pruning it hard—it will just flower later than normal or, in the case of an old shrub rose that only flowers on the previous year's growth, it may skip a year (in which case, you shouldn't prune it again until after it has flowered).

2. While remembering the names of your roses is unimportant, knowing their basic type is vital so that you can learn how and when to prune them. Broadly put, bush roses, modern shrubs (such as the Hybrid Musks and English Roses previously mentioned), Rugosas and climbers (that flower on new wood) should be pruned in late winter. Old shrub roses and ramblers (that flower on shoots produced the previous year) need shortening soon after flowering.

3. Ramblers (the prickly beasts that produce huge shoots every year in late summer on which they flower just once the following June) really do need big trees to climb up. Anywhere else and their maintenance is a nightmare. Much more manageable climbers are a far better choice for arches, fences, pergolas and house walls. The labels on roses always make the distinction between the two clear.

4. Never thread a rose through a trellis as both

trellis and rose will suffer. Tie it on instead, using soft and stretchy Flexi-Tie.

5. I hardly dare say this, but regrettably roses will not fulfil their potential unless they are sprayed to keep them healthy, fed every year and pruned properly. Apart from the Rugosas, they are not 'easy'.

6. And finally, the best, full-on, over-the-top totally unforgettable rosy experience is to be had by visiting Mottisfont Abbey Garden in Hampshire, a glorious walled garden, home to the National Collection of old roses, late on a hot afternoon in June (when most other visitors have gone home).

SEDUM PESTS

Sedums, those old border favourites, have had a bit of a re-birth recently. They seem so stout, fleshy and prolific that it may surprise those whose gardens seem to be overrun with the old stand-by *Sedum spectabile* to hear that they can be problematic in any way. However, Peter from Basingstoke wants to know how to avoid his being eaten by numerous small caterpillars that made 'mincemeat' of them last year, spinning fine webs over the shoot tips and destroying the flower buds.

These are the caterpillars of the ermine moth that operates by night, laying eggs on various ornamental plants and particularly favouring sedums. The only way to beat this one is to spray with a systemic insecticide now, before the moth is active, thereby rendering the sedums unpalatable to the tiny caterpillars as they hatch out. Provado Ultimate Bug Killer, which contains thiacloprid, should do the trick.

DEATH OF A VIBURNUM

In late spring last year I noticed that the leaves of my beautiful **Viburnum plicatum tomentosum** *'Mariesii' had failed to expand, and by June it was clear that it had died. A new shoot appeared from the soil about 18in (45cm) away from the main plant. When I dug up and destroyed the dead plant I detached this shoot and some root and potted them up. What caused the main plant to die, and can I now replant the healthy offspring?*
Janet, East Sussex

I had a similar problem a few years ago. Apparently, the cause of death is very likely to have been a deadly phytophthora infection, to which many ornamental trees and shrubs are prone, particularly in wet soils. Phytophthora spores are frequently found in garden soil, but not all plants succumb. I presume you have the infamous Wadhurst clay underlying your garden soil. Plants that are grown in nurseries in soil-less composts and then planted in heavy soil like yours are likely to become waterlogged and this can encourage infection, a point worth noting for the future.

The new shoot was produced from a part of the root that survived the attack, so you could replant the surviving portion, but there is always a risk that it will go the same way as its parent, particularly if you put it in the same spot.

JOHNSON'S BLUES

I was very disappointed when the **Geranium** *'Johnson's Blue' that I bought and planted last autumn turned out to be nothing like the geraniums of that name that I admired in a garden in Somerset last year. Is it possible that the flower colour could be affected by soil pH or other growing conditions?*
Naomi, Peterborough

In some plants (most notably hydrangeas) soil pH does affect flower colour. However, as I am sure you know, there are numerous varieties of blue herbaceous geranium, some of them barely distinguishable from one another, and while I am sure it was not deliberate, I imagine you have been sold the wrong geranium. It is impossible to know what is what when all you are buying are dormant plants that are no more than black plastic pots full of soil with just a label.

I suspect you have acquired *Geranium himalayense* 'Gravetye', with which 'Johnson's Blue' is so often confused. There are numerous botanical differences between this and the much-admired 'Johnson's Blue', but

84

both flower at around the same time, are approximately the same size and are both 'blue'. Well, sort of. If you see the two together it is quite obvious which is the real McCoy. But if you have nothing with which to compare yours directly, you have to do the See-Through Test, as I call it. Nip off a flower and hold it up to the light. The real JB has not got one jot or iota of pink in its heavenly, transparent, luminous lavender/grey flowers—which is precisely why it is so special—while its (to my mind) inferior cousin has flowers that are veined in vivid magenta when held up to the light.

If indeed you have got 'Gravetye', then shunt it off to the shade somewhere, where it will do extremely well, flowering off and on to the autumn. Try again with 'Johnson's Blue'—perhaps beg a piece from a reliable source, having first done the See-Through Test of course. Come to think of it, this is something we could all bore our friends with for years to come…

HEMEROCALLIS DISAPPOINTMENT

Why do most of the buds on my day lilies (I do not know the variety, but they are the normal pale orange ones) swell up and fail to open? The problem seems to be getting worse each year. I would like to plant some of the more interesting-coloured varieties but would hate them to catch the same disease.
Frances, Roehampton

I get a variation on this letter each year. But I will pass on the encouraging news that I have managed to completely solve this nasty, disappointing problem in my own garden.

The swollen buds are the work of the hemerocallis gall midge, a minuscule fly that lays its eggs on the flower buds of day lilies after they emerge from the soil in early summer. When the eggs hatch the larvae feast on the buds—if you open one up you may find tiny white grubs inside. After the damaged buds drop, the grubs pupate over winter in the soil, and the cycle starts again.

Your first task in the war against this beast should be to remove all the swollen buds so that you automatically interrupt its life cycle. Cultivate the soil around the base of the plants with a small fork during the winter to disturb any stray cocoons, and next year you could spray the plants with Provado Ultimate Bug Killer—a systemic and contact insecticide—as the buds start to appear in mid-May. You may be lucky enough to catch any survivors before they do their worst, but if not you will render the plant inhospitable to their grubs.

RHODODENDRON QUERIES

A clutch of rhododendron questions. Jane from Hertfordshire wants to know whether there is something wrong with some of hers. She has noticed that they have slightly furry backs to their leaves. No cause for panic—this cinnamon-coloured 'fur' (known as indumentum) is quite normal on Japanese yakushima rhododendrons. Black, bristly buds that disappointingly fail to open, however, such as those present in ever-increasing numbers on Bob's rhododendrons, are not such good news. This is rhododendron bud blast—a fungal disease spread by colonies of an exotic-looking leafhopper that flits around the bushes in the hottest part of the summer. The only way to defeat the disease is to remove and destroy as many of the blackened buds as possible, and then wage war on the leafhopper with an insecticide (Provado Ultimate Bug Killer might do the trick).

New gardener Maya's rhodies are getting a bit too big for their boots, and her garden is tiny. Can she 'snip them back a bit' to keep them in check? And should she deadhead them to get rid of the ugly old flower heads?

These are loaded questions. Yes, it is possible to prune rhododendrons—quite hard if you have to. They will come back smiling eventually, but they may take their time—a couple of years even—to start flowering well again. If, however, you tweak at them just a little every year, shortening all the branches to neaten them up as Maya hints that she would like to do, you may end up continually cutting off the shoots that would flower the following year. A compromise has to be found—possibly in the complete removal of any particularly lanky branches every other year, and minimal disturbance of the rest of each bush. As for deadheading: in the case of very large bushes in large gardens this is clearly not a practical option—and anyway once the petals have fallen and new growth has covered up all that scruffiness,

87

it is hardly a pressing visual problem when viewed from a distance. In the case of smaller bushes that are very much in your face in a small garden, then teasing off each spent flower head with finger and thumb tidies things up considerably. What Maya mustn't do is use secateurs, since it is all too easy to snip off the newest buds developing at the base of the old flower head.

CISTUSES—PRUNE OR NOT?

I have several cistuses in an open, sunny part of my garden given over to mainly Mediterranean plants. They have all done very well but I was advised when I put them in eight years ago that I should not prune them. One of them in particular (with sticky leaves and large white flowers) is looking tired and thin, while some of the others have spread sideways and are each covering several square feet. If I cut them back, will I lose them, as I was led to believe?
Meryl, by email

Eight years is quite an age for a cistus, and some of yours, particularly the kind you describe as now being 'thin', have probably more or less burnt themselves out and should be replaced. None of the largest, woody cistuses (such as *Cistus ladanifer*) respond well if you cut into them severely in order to 'renovate' them. Others, however, could be controlled by pruning and some of yours may come back full strength for another year or two. For example, large-flowered, lax and leafy *C. × purpureus* and *C.* 'Alan Fradd'

88

(with pink, and white maroon-blotched flowers respectively) can both be pruned immediately after they have flowered (you can remove as much as 2ft/60cm, cutting down to a pair of tiny shoots). Smaller-flowered varieties, such as the extremely wide-spreading *C. × skanbergii* and *C. × corbariensis,* can have their excessively sprawling extremities removed completely and the rest of the shoots that have borne flowers shortened a little.

If you go over all your bushes immediately after flowering you will know by the end of the summer whether they have enough oomph left to recover their looks and flower another year. If they still look ugly by October, heave them out, replenish the soil with a little grit and compost and plant new bushes next spring.

VIBURNUM BEETLE

I grow **Viburnum opulus** *mainly for its autumn colour and scarlet berries and don't take much notice of it at this time of year. However, I was shocked to notice that the shrub has completely nibbled leaves—some have small holes in them, others are reduced almost to shreds. I can't see anything actually doing the damage: has it done the deed and flown away? What action should I take?*
Jane, Dagenham, Essex

The leaf nibbling and shredding is the work of the grubs of a nasty pest, the viburnum beetle, that also commonly attacks the popular evergreen *Viburnum tinus*. These larvae may indeed have already vanished from view but they are not far away— pupating in the soil beneath the shrub. They will duly emerge in a month or so as hungry adult beetles and will feed on the foliage of the host shrub until early autumn and deposit their eggs on its woody stems. These will overwinter and hatch next spring, and so the merry-go-round continues—unless you take action, that is.

There really is not a lot you can do at the moment. I am told that lightly cultivating the soil beneath the shrubs to disturb and reveal the pupae is tempting to do but not necessarily effective—unless perhaps you have a hopelessly tame robin virtually sitting on your shoulder while you do it. To save your shrub (since repeated attacks that go unchecked could eventually kill it) and in an attempt to interrupt the life cycle of the beetle, you should try to catch the adults as— or even before—they do damage in late summer by spraying with a systemic-and-contact spray containing thiacloprid, such as Provado Ultimate Bug Killer. Not the sort of job you want to be doing on a lazy late summer evening, but if needs must… And next spring, as the leaves unfurl, have another go with the spray bottle in case you missed a few baddies and a new generation of larvae are on the prowl. This is one you can win, with a bit of effort.

HONEY FUNGUS

Often prefaced by 'the dreaded', the very words honey fungus send shudders down the spine. I get numerous letters and emails from people who have experienced more than one unexplained death of a tree or shrub, generally suspect the worst and want to know how to arrest the spread or put off the arrival of this nasty fungal disease.

Symptoms are well documented: sudden, rapid wilting of the foliage of a mature tree or shrub, often at the height of the growing season, followed by death; the appearance of groups of orange toadstools, often—but not always—at the base of an old tree; the presence of long dark rhizomorphs (the famous 'bootlaces') in the soil, by which the fungus travels from a host plant to its 'prey'; and tell-tale white fungal growth underneath bark.

Here are some facts that may enlighten or reassure:

1. If you have honey fungus at large in your garden, you cannot 'cure' it, and there are no chemicals to control it. You can merely hope to manage it and work around it.

2. You should, however, never leave a dead woody plant sitting around. Dig it up with as much root as possible and dispose of it.

3. Well-fed plants with healthy growing conditions are less likely to be attacked than those that are waterlogged, droughted or otherwise under stress.

4. Not all groups of yellow toadstools are honey fungus. The real McCoy has a distinct collar around its stalk. Brushing away the toadstools won't brush away the problem. The fungus is more often spread by the 'bootlaces'.

5. There are various different types of honey fungus; some are not as virulent as others, but some plants—privet, apple trees, roses and viburnums, for example—are particularly susceptible. Since the bootlaces travel in the top few inches of soil, physical barriers, such as a vertical strip of butyl rubber, can quite effectively protect plants that are growing close to a suspected source of disease.

DEALING WITH BINDWEED

Completely new to gardening, I have recently discovered that my garden is full of bindweed, which is now twining over the surface of most of my shrubs and roses. Help!
Michael, Kent

This may look like an insurmountable problem, but it is not. I managed to cleanse an entire infested flowerbed in my garden in one season. You need to get in there and carefully untwine as much of the bindweed as possible from your bushes without breaking it off from its roots. Stuff it into a plastic bag and spray glyphosate weedkiller such as Roundup extremely carefully into the bag, making sure that all the foliage within is saturated. Knot the handles of the bag together and stuff the bags out of sight under the shrubs. I have also in my time done a nifty trick by dipping a rubber-gloved hand in a bowl of glyphosate mix, grabbing a handful of untangled bindweed shoots with the gloved hand, taking the glove off (therefore turning it inside out) and burying the glove full of bindweed temporarily in the soil until the deed is done. This last trick was extremely quick and easy to do, but it was a little disconcerting to discover a series of old rubber gloves in the soil a few months later.

Glyphosate kills weeds by travelling downwards to the extensive, often brittle roots of perennial weeds and killing them. The process takes about two weeks. There may be some re-growth, and there will of course be bits that get missed, but a repeat treatment later in the season should do the trick.

HOLLYHOCKS AND RUST

Hollyhocks are one of my favourite garden flowers. Is there any way of dealing with the rust that affects mine? And in areas where plants have succumbed to rust and died, is it safe to plant new ones, or will the soil be contaminated?
Stella, Sussex

First I should say that one way to 'deal' with hollyhock rust is to treat your plants (officially short-lived perennials) more or less as biennials—and ditch them after a couple of years before they start to go downhill because of (almost inevitable) rust. If you let some of your plants go to seed you will find new little plants crop up regularly and while they are small can be relocated or potted up.

93

By struggling to keep old plants going you may do more harm than good, merely increasing the risk of other nearby younger hollyhocks becoming infected by spores of this fungal disease.

There are certainly practical steps you can take to minimise the spread of the disease, even if you don't want to use chemicals. The most effective of these is to remove all the plant's lower leaves as the stems power upwards in early summer. It is these leaves that invariably show the first signs of infection (rusty-coloured spots on their undersides), and their removal considerably slows down the progress of the whole thing— it apparently has a lot to do with preventing rain splashing the spores up on to higher foliage. As for chemical control: I have also managed, in addition to leaf removal, to control rust to great effect by spraying with a systemic fungicide such as Systhane Fungus Fighter, early on in the season, and repeating the process a few weeks later.

And contaminated soil? In theory fungal spores hang around in the soil for some time. However you have to take a pragmatic view, I think. Cultivate the soil well and incorporate some muck/compost and/or a little general fertiliser each time you replace your plants; take the steps outlined above and clear away any infected foliage promptly and just carry on. If you adore hollyhocks and want to grow them in a specific place, then hollyhocks in that specific place you simply must have.

PLANTS FOR A TINY BOG GARDEN

I have built a stupidly small pond, 6ft 4in (1.9m) in diameter. My bog garden consists of an old wicker shopping basket put in one corner. I have common sedge (a waste of space, I feel) and early purple orchids growing nearby. What else can I grow, and how shall I manage the area?
Anita, by email

Firstly, don't be so hard on yourself. A six foot pond is not 'stupidly small'. Any piece of still water in a garden that can sustain life will attract insect and bird life, and can make an interesting habitat for moisture-loving plants. I think the current fad for all-singing-all-dancing 'water features' with lights, spiral cascades and bits of bamboo that go bump in the night is just that. A fad.

When I lived in London I had a pre-formed plastic pond not much bigger than yours. It was teeming with frogs, water boatmen and all sorts of interesting creatures, and buzzed with dragonflies. With its back edge tucked into a bank of shrubs, which provided cover for wildlife, I daubed the front edges of the grey plastic (where it showed) with a non-toxic brownish wood stain, and 'faked' a bog garden by digging out a patch of soil (about 2 cubic feet/0.06 cubic metres) next to the end that overflowed when it rained hard. I lined this with an offcut of butyl rubber pond liner, pierced it in a couple of places and filled it with some ericaceous compost mixed with grit. In this I grew early summer-flowering *Iris sibirica* and some wonderful red and orange candelabra primulas, and later-flowering *Primula florindae* (which smells deliciously of dried ginger), only needing to water it occasionally in mid-summer. Get rid of the sedge: as you say, it is a waste of precious space and a bit of a thug in a small area. I do hope your little pond thrives—I am sure you will get a lot of enjoyment from it, as I did from mine.

FASCIATION

Joy from Morpeth sent me a picture of an extraordinary white foxglove, the topmost flower of which had opened out into a dramatic white 'ruff'—quite unlike the rest of its flowers—and asks if she has a new weird and wonderful hybrid on her hands.

Alas, this is just a manifestation of a condition called fasciation that affects numerous garden plants. I understand it is caused by slight damage to growing tips—by slugs or insects or even frost—in their early stages of development. Hence weird appearances such as Joy's foxglove flower, or flattened and contorted, triffid-like stems on other verticals such as verbascums and delphiniums and also on woody plants such as forsythia. If growths are unsightly they should simply be removed. If not, you can always take pictures and marvel at them—as Joy did.

UNFAIR COMPETITION

A certain Bicester gentleman—if indeed you can call him that—is up to no good. He is competing with a couple of nine-year-olds (shame on him, couldn't he pick someone his own size?) to whom he gave some seedlings of Russian Giant sunflowers, to see who can grow them the tallest. He now wants some tips on how to win. Maxicrop Plant Growth Stimulant, shelter from the wind— and a stout stake for each plant. And (if it is not too late) he should slip a large black plastic plant pot with the bottom removed and some copper sticky tape around its girth over the head of each of his plants and press them into the soil a little, just in case his young rivals go around collecting all the fattest, hungriest snails they can find in the neighbourhood and unleash them in his garden. Personally I wouldn't blame them if they did, would you?

July

THE HAMPTON COURT HACK

If you missed out on (or could not bear to do) the Chelsea Chop, then why don't you try the Hampton Court Hack? For those who need an explanation, I will attempt one. The Chelsea Chop—so called because it is customarily carried out at the end of May at Chelsea Flower Show time—is a method by which you delay and/or prolong the flowering season of many herbaceous plants, while at the same time reducing their height and persuading them to flower better, by cutting them down by as much as half (see May, page 47). Depending on the particular candidate in question and the desired effect, all the stems, some of the stems or even one whole side of plants can be treated in this way. For soft-hearted and impatient gardeners, it is extremely hard to bring oneself to lop off (to give just one example) the lovely emerging pink cabbagey buds of sedums just as they are beginning to play their part in the overall summer tableau. However, the consequences (in due course) are dramatic: sturdier plants and even more flowers.

I was my usual lily-livered self, and despite good intentions only cut down those plants that I knew to be so unruly by nature that they would otherwise be impossible to grow in my confined space. But everything grew and grew and (however well supported) fell over. In early July (around Hampton Court Flower Show time) I was forced to go around my entire garden and cut things

99

back—if not exactly ruthlessly, at least bravely. Barrowload after barrowload of super-lush foliage and damaged flower stems were carted off to compost bins. Surprisingly, the garden prospered and definitely looked better for longer, only a few sun-starved annuals failing to get into their stride.

The real success story was the Russian sage, *Perovskia* 'Blue Spire', a lovely grey, aromatic-leaved sub-shrub with late, blue flower spikes and skeletal white winter stems, which resolutely refuses to stand to attention in all but complete, all round, all-year-round sunshine, with which few of our gardens are blessed. Perovskia is slow to start in the spring and needs to be cut back to a low woody framework once the frosts have truly finished. By Chelsea Chop time, it has barely made any growth. But if pruned in late spring as described and then given the Hampton Court Hack in July, it may, like mine, produce numerous perfectly orderly erect blue flower heads in early September. (There is a smaller variety, 'Little Spire', that will grow straighter, but in my view it is not up to much.) The Hampton Court Hack may be just as painful as the Chelsea Chop but the results will be rewarding. If nothing else, have a go at your astrantias—you will be amazed.

WATER SHORTAGE

We gardeners should have geared up for crisis summers by installing water butts wherever possible and hopefully we will not have to go to extremes and start diverting our old bath water. But we should get our priorities sorted out and be ready to water our gardens sensibly 'by hand'. As the going gets tough, the following guidelines may be helpful.

- Never water the lawn. It will recover by September. Yes, it really will.
- Save your best watering efforts for newly planted trees and shrubs. Water in the evening, very thoroughly, aiming the water carefully at the base of plants, not at the leaves. Make a shallow circular gully in the soil approximately in line with the outermost branches of vulnerable trees and shrubs in which to pour water every few days. You can also use moisture-retaining mulches of compost or composted bark, scraping them back before you water and replacing afterwards.
- Packed borders seem to suffer less in great heat than sparsely planted ones, which may seem somewhat illogical until you consider the fact that the soil is shielded from the worst of the heat by all the foliage and flowers. In extreme heat, only water border plants that are new or are still wilting in the evening. Resolve to become less dependent on thirsty annuals, and if you simply have to plant something new (and sometimes this just can't be avoided for all sorts of reasons), do so in the evening, drenching the plant before you start by standing it in a bucket of water till the bubbles no longer rise. Fill planting holes with water and let them drain, but earth the new plants up with dry soil and don't water at all for a few days, in order to encourage them to start putting roots down, not up.
- Plants in containers can be potted up with moisture-retaining gel, and seem to fare better

(and are less likely to get missed out when watering) if grouped together—this is particularly important if you are asking someone else to water them for you in your absence.

- Finally, since we will have to use them daily, the choice of watering can is important. I find that a pair of oval-shaped plastic cans with a single handle over the top (as beloved traditionally by the French and now readily available here) is easier to carry and pour from than the traditional cylindrical two-handled English-style ones. These just bang into your legs, slop into your slippers, have to be carried uncomfortably, ape-style with hands facing forward—and are impossible to use one handed. I also particularly recommend a push-button can, which is lightweight and completely controllable. Inevitably, I fear, we will all develop shoulders like Amazons by the end of the summer.

GRAVEL WITHOUT TEARS

Frank is about to embark on creating a low-maintenance gravelled area on what is currently a rather dry, sunny piece of lawn. Should he use a weed-smothering membrane?

Whether or not to use a membrane depends, I think, on what kind of land is being converted and—almost as importantly—your interpretation of the magic words 'low maintenance'. If you use a membrane you need to control the weeds with a weedkiller before you start, and be certain that the worst of the baddies are well and truly seen off before you put it down. You can always put a layer of sand as a buffer between the membrane and the gravel on specific pathways in order to make them less skiddy, and this can be zapped with a contact product such as Weedol that will 'burn' away any weeds as soon as they appear. If you do enough preparation, then the membrane does enable you to have a low-maintenance garden. But the garden can end up looking a bit blobby and unrelaxed, and gives limited scope for change and natural expansion. This is just my view, of course. Others may find it looks chic and minimalist.

Frank may decide not to use a membrane: he could just remove old turf (or weedkill or dig up a threadbare lawn), dig in some muck or compost, and plant whatever he chooses, before covering the ground with a soil-obliterating layer of gravel. In which case he will probably have to settle for a good few years of weeding anyway, since the gravel will not stop subsequent germination of all sorts of undesirables that are lurking in the soil—mostly grass and perennial lawn weeds that he may have missed. Gravel on much-trodden areas will have to be topped up every year or so.

The good part about a membrane-less gravel garden is that you can add and subtract, divide and multiply as time goes on. The whole thing becomes joined-up and lush very quickly. The bad news is that if you don't know your seedlings from your weedlings things can get a bit tense after a year or so, and 'low maintenance' it isn't. In early spring you may have to 'weed out' all sorts of lovely things that have gone berserk, and just getting the hang of what constitutes 'berserk' is an acquired skill in itself.

A GARDENER'S PLEA

The next few weeks can present us country gardeners with an enormous challenge—for we are about to be invaded. I write not of marching knotweed, armies of pollen beetles or droning columns of leather-clad weekend bikers, but of our own dear town-dwelling friends. 'Do come and stay, why don't you, when the weather cheers up?' 'Oh my god, they are actually coming. Bang goes another weekend's gardening... and I bet they will bring us another bloody rose.'

Here follows a plea to all visiting gift horses that would rather not be looked in the mouth. Please, please, don't, in the mistaken belief that we will be delighted, bring us a tree, a shrub, a rose, or anything that needs immediate attention and lots of space. If you simply must bring us a plant, ask us first what we would like, for while it is wonderful to be given something one has hankered after but cannot afford or cannot source locally, it is quite another thing to be landed with a randomly chosen, space-hungry shrub that will have to be found a home and nurtured until your next visit. And especially please don't hunt for the most rare, most tender thing you can find on the grounds that if we are serious gardeners we want something 'special'. If you simply must bring a pot of something, make it bland, easy and temporary—rather than some Australian horticultural fancy we have never heard of that needs its hand held at night.

So what would we appreciate? This question is usually wheeled out for Christmas, but is far more pressing an issue in the summer, when ghastly mistakes are so often made.

If potted hardy plants are a bit of a no-no (although I suspect the tender perennial *Argyranthemum* 'Jamaica Primrose' would please even die-hard yellowphobes), unless you know for a fact that your hostess has done the full Sarah-Raven-Cutting-Garden monty, then cut flowers are welcome, especially if tastefully pre-bunched and in water. Forget the carrying coals to Newcastle cliché: many of us are loath to raid our own borders to decorate the house.

Tools should be seriously smart. No one can possibly complain if they are given an extra pair of Felco secateurs, a Sneeboer hand fork or a posh canvas kneeler from The Carrier Company. Expensive gardeners' hand cream will go down a storm. But otherwise go easy on the smelly, pampering stuff. You don't want to imply that your hostess's hands are wrecked and/or she needs to take more frequent relaxing baths. This may well be the case, but you are not supposed to notice. Cheap gardening gloves (especially silly floral things) are hateful, as are folksy gardening aprons and anything with 'head gardener' or 'under gardener' written on it. A bottle of Pimm's is probably a better idea.

If you want to get real brownie points, remember that we will have given up precious gardening time for odious housework, bed-making and so on. One of the nicest things you could do is offer to work for us. Any guest of mine who sweeps paths, weeds between the shallots or cleans greenhouse windows with me is a friend for life. And who knows, they might be bitten by the bug, move out of their horrid smelly cities, buy their own patch of rabbit-infested ground elder and start to understand.

SPECTACULAR EUPHORBIA

I would welcome some advice about how to treat a spectacular **Euphorbia characias** *subsp.* **wulfenii,** *which cheers up my garden in spring and early summer. It has become rather leggy and I need to know when and how it should be pruned. Also, what is the best way to propagate it?*
Julia, Ely

I have never quite understood why some people have such an aversion to huge, almost shrubby euphorbias such as this one, since their stems and foliage have a useful year-round presence and, as you say, their enormous lime green heads can illuminate a garden even on a dull day. They have a relatively short life, however, and your leggy specimen may have passed its best.

To keep shrubby euphorbias going and looking good for as long as possible, they should have their old flower heads cut right out at the base each year as they fade in June or July, leaving just one (for reasons that will become clear). By cutting out the developing seed heads you will channel the plants' energies into the stout crop of new stems that will already be formed, but will not have flowered. Merely deadheading the old shoots will encourage them to branch and produce two smaller flower heads, which rather spoil the look of the plant the following year. I feed and mulch the bases of my big euphorbias each spring, and give them a liquid feed after I have cut out the old stems. Each autumn you can tell which of the shoots are going to produce flowers—they start to bend over rather curiously. I have found that some of my euphorbias—both these and a little ground-hugging relation, *E. myrsenitis*— have suffered from a fungal leaf spot that makes the lower part of the stems defoliate. A systemic fungicide such as Systhane applied to the new growth should clear this up.

As for propagation, I have always found that seedlings pop up quite frequently as a result of leaving that one remaining flower head (technically a mass of bracts surrounding tiny flowers and seeds that you can actually hear exploding on hot days). The seedlings should be potted up while young and cosseted a little before being put in a permanent site. These euphorbias have coarse roots that do not readily make a good root ball, and therefore do not transplant easily. Books will tell you that it is possible to take stem cuttings in spring, but I find that because of the plant's extremely leaky (and irritant) sap, this is less rewarding than hanging around waiting for seedlings.

FLOPPY CATMINT

Pamela from Cambridgeshire sent me a photograph of an enormous floppy catmint given to her 20 years ago. Unfortunately she has 'lost' it since her cat used to roll in it too vigorously during the summer. She wonders if I know its name so that she can buy a new one and try again. From the picture it looked like the notoriously unruly *Nepeta* 'Six Hills Giant'. Pamela might like to try a similarly large variety, 'Walker's Low', which in my experience is a little less likely to flop. You can support catmint and protect it from determined nibbling and lolling cats, to a degree, by putting an upside-down hanging basket over the top of each plant in early spring. Those who have missed the bus, as it were, for this year, could put basket(s) in place when they take the shears to nepeta just after its first flowering flush around July. The second showing of this repeat-flowering lovely blowsy thing should then be protected. Boot fairs and junk shops are a good source of old baskets.

HEAT AND DUST

My two-year-old 'Star of India' clematis has some mildew-type grey dust on some of its lower shoots and some of the leaves are starting to die. The upper parts of the plant are growing well. It is on a south-facing wall. I cut it down in the autumn after it had flowered brilliantly last summer.
John, Cheadle, Staffordshire

108

'Star of India' clematis is a lovely, generally reliable thing, with large, late summer-flowering purple flowers, each petal of which is banded in deep red. You are right in thinking that your plant has a touch of mildew, and I think your problem with it stems from the fact that it is planted against a hot south-facing wall. Mildew frequently attacks plants that are dry at the roots. Last year you may have taken great steps to see that it was watered adequately because it was new and special (we all do that), and this year the south-facing wall may have become a giant storage radiator just when the plant was starting to put on all its new growth. To try to rescue the situation give it a huge drench of water—2 gallons (9 litres) at least—applied very slowly to a wide area all around the base. You could add some soluble plant food to the water to pep things up. Follow this up by applying a thick organic mulch of some sort—home-made compost, well-rotted manure, composted bark or leaf mould. Also spray the entire plant with a systemic fungicide such as Systhane to try to control the mildew. Thereafter water the plant every fortnight or so, scraping back and replacing the mulch, and topping it up if necessary.

Clematis plants are frequently tricky for a year or two until established, and almost always complain (by getting mildew or just giving up the ghost) when planted in hot places—particularly if there is nothing nearby that will shade their roots from mid-day sun. Once established, they rarely need a lot of

TLC, but perhaps you could plant a strategic shrub in front of yours—but not so close as to present it with serious competition for available moisture. Or, if you planted it too close to the wall in the first place—less than 18in (45cm) away—you would do well to keep it going as best you can this summer, and move it in the autumn.

Whatever you do, do not make the incredibly common mistake of thinking that a couple of old roof tiles or bits of broken plant pot are sufficient to keep the roots of clematis cool. They are absolutely not.

A CASE OF REVERSION

Five years ago I planted a fuchsia with pretty pink, cream and grey-green leaves. I cut it back each spring (as advised by you a long time ago), which makes it a neat, side-spreading bush. However, although it still flowers well it is gradually getting less interesting because more and more of the shoots are turning up with green leaves, even though I cut these green shoots back as I believe you should.
Chloe, by email

Variegated and coloured-leaved plants such as this are basically attractive 'freaks' that have been propagated especially for their freakishness. With some, it would seem, the whole thing is quite fragile and the plants are capable of reverting back to their old original green state. Variegated acers, euonymus and eleagnus are just two of the worst offenders that spring to mind—and of course, this particularly beautiful fuchsia is pretty tricky—but other shrubs seem to be fine. I have never, for example, had a problem with a variegated pittosporum reverting in this way.

The green shoots are naturally more vigorous than the coloured shoots since they contain more chlorophyll, and will eventually start to dominate the plants and even take over completely. Cutting back reverted green shoots in these circumstances sometimes makes the problem worse, since if you prune out only half the offending branch, it may immediately make more new all-green shoots from the axils of lower leaves. The safer course of action is to cut cleanly back to the main stem from which the green shoots come. However, you may find that your fuchsia has just gone too far. It may be easier to replace it. You could try propagating from some of the remaining coloured stems: nip off a few soft, flower-less shoots in late summer; remove lower leaves; pot them in a very sandy compost and keep them covered and in the shade. Or—simpler if you have a couple of brass farthings to spare—dig up the old plant, buy a new one and armed with this information, keep an eye open for the first sign of reversion in the future.

POLLEN BEETLES

Scores of small black beetles, smaller than a ladybird but bigger than a flea, crawled in droves out of the sweet peas I picked and brought into the house. Where have they come from? Will they spread to other flowers and how, please, can I get rid of them?
Glen, by email

Don't panic. These are pollen beetles and the trouble they cause only lasts for a few weeks in early summer. They breed profusely on brassica plants, members of the cabbage family, of which of course oil seed rape is one. I suspect you may live in an area where farm crop rotation has given you a field of this yellow-flowered plant nearby. The vast population of pollen beetles in fields naturally spills over into local gardens once the larvae have hatched, and the beetles home in on other flowers to gorge on their pollen.

It is no use spraying the flowers with an insecticide—and this would harm beneficial pollinating insects anyway. All you can do, if you are under attack from these annoying pests, is shake your cut flowers gently once you have picked them, then put them in water in a dark place such as a garage or garden shed, where there is just a little light coming from a small window. The beetles are attracted to light and so will leave the flowers within a few hours, after which it is safer to bring them indoors.

AN IRIS QUERY

Should I be doing something to my irises this month? They have been growing and flowering quite well at the base of a sunny wall for two years. I seem to remember that my grandfather, who grew them in his rose beds, always cut their leaves down in the middle of the summer. Was this just to tidy them up?
Phillip, by email

I am assuming that these are the handsome-flowered bearded irises that grow from knobbly-looking rhizomes. These make a striking spring/early summer show in traditional rose gardens, where the rose bushes are pruned down quite low each winter. Your grandfather would have cut the iris leaves back after they had flowered just as the new rose shoots grew in stature, in order that the iris rhizomes would get as much direct sun as possible. Without direct sun they would flower poorly the following year. Strictly speaking, if your irises are not shaded by other plants and are in a hot, sunny site, you do not need to cut the leaves back (which I think makes them rather ugly), although you can remove any older leaves that are dying off.

July is the time, however, to divide irises when their matted rhizomes become less productive—which yours will in the next year or so. They should be dug up, the outermost rhizomes kept and the oldest, central part of the mat discarded. Having trimmed the leaves, replant the saved sections horizontally, about 6–8in (15–20cm) apart, with the rooty end of each to the south and the leaves to the north (it is all about direct sun again). Rake some bonemeal into the soil before you plant, but don't give them much nitrogen-rich food, and don't cover them with soil or overwater them. These irises do rather better if you are a bit mean to them.

UNCOMMON SCENTS

Emailer Wendy Albright asks me to recommend some unusual plants that are strongly scented on summer nights. She already grows night-scented stock and tobacco plants from seed, and has pots of lilies and a lovely *Philadelphus* 'Sybille' under her bedroom window.

There are loads of night-time smellies, of course, and with the minimum of brain-wracking I have come up with the following: a tenderish shrub *Cestrum parqui*, with small, lime-green flowers that are nothing to write home about during the day, but at night give off a really heady sweet-shop scent; the evergreen climber *Trachelospermum jasminoides* (about which I have enthused before). To grow from seed: *Mirabilis jalapa*, the four o'clock plant, has garish colours and heavy scent, and makes a tuber almost as hardy as a dahlia; the white shrubby perennial stock, *Matthiola incana alba*; and another little winner, an annual with an impossible name: *Zaluzianskya capensis* (named after Adam Zaluziansky von Zaluzian—yes, really). A friend gave me a plant she had raised from seed and its night scent is just gorgeous.

114

FOXGLOVES

I thought that once common-or-garden biennial foxgloves (Digitalis purpurea) had flowered they died, so I pull mine up at the end of the summer. I notice, however, that some of my plants have got what looks like new growth appearing underneath the old tatty leaves at the bottom of the stem. If I just cut them down, will they flower a second year?
Denise, by email

Some will, some won't. I have not yet managed to fathom out quite what makes some foxgloves go that extra lap. Some of the stoutest of mine, planted in the best soil, collapse after flowering as you might expect, while others, ostensibly less happy plants, carry on. Perhaps that is the answer. The paltry specimens feel that they have not done a decent enough job at creating the next generation by only producing a squillion seeds (whereas a decent plant will of course produce at least two squillion seeds), so hangs on to life to have another go.

On a more practical note: I would cut down the plants that are showing signs of new growth, water them and firm their roots into the ground (the plants may have been top heavy and loosened themselves in the soil). Sometimes, I find, these plants do go on to produce a new healthy rosette of leaves and flower quite well a second year. But just as many get mildew and generally fail to thrive, so that in spring you end up chucking them out anyway. I always add to my natural foxglove population each year—planting one-year-old seedlings of white ones and of 'Sutton's Apricot' (which a friend raises from seed for me), to combine with those wild pink ones that have self-seeded to create a mixed-coloured population. The colours are getting more interesting and varied every year.

While we're on the subject, I've had emails from gardeners who can't seem to get foxgloves to self-seed, especially where they want them to. I can almost see all those eyebrows shooting up—while some gardeners adore them, grand gardeners get very snooty about foxgloves, regarding them as frightful weeds. Anyway, their tiny, very vulnerable seedlings can easily be annihilated by slugs, raked or hoed out before they make their presence felt. The ones that do progress to the leafy stage can get hoiked out with all the other 'unwanteds'. Thus the more neat and tidy you are about the garden, the less likely foxgloves are to establish themselves—except in crevices and between paving stones where they avoid attention.

A little subtle manipulation is needed. I learned a useful trick when I started cultivating the woodland margins in my old, country garden: I used to cut whole foxglove stems down just as they were about to drop their seed, shake out the seeds in areas that I wanted them to colonise, and then lie the very noticeable stems around on the ground as a useful reminder to me not to walk over the area or disturb the ground for several months. Once the seedlings were big enough to handle, I thinned them out and moved them around. Within two years, the wood was absolutely awash with glorious foxgloves of all colours.

Is there another lesson to learn from this, apart from the need for stage management? Yes, I think so. Of all the many skills we gardeners have to acquire, learning the difference between one's seedlings and one's weedlings is probably one of the most important.

RUGOSA HEDGE

Last year we planted a long row of 17 Rugosa rose bushes to make, ultimately, a low hedge between two areas of garden. There are now numerous suckers appearing from the base of the bushes and also springing up in the ground around them. To make a thick hedge, should these suckers be cut or allowed to grow?
Heather, Porthmadog, Gwynedd

One of the reasons these robust, disease-free roses are used for hedging is that they flower throughout most of the summer, producing highly scented blooms followed (almost always) by round luscious-looking red or orange hips the size of cherry tomatoes. These last for a couple of months before withering and providing splendid food for wild birds. Most Rugosas grow from their own roots which sucker naturally, bulking out

117

the hedge and eventually flowering, helping to make the hedge, ultimately, quite simple to maintain. (Suckers from roses grafted on to wild rose roots are clearly different—see Sports and Suckers, page 121.) Broadly speaking, you should leave the suckers alone. Some of those that start to grow towards the end of the summer may not have much substance to them and—if you feel like grappling around in the undergrowth—you could remove them to encourage the production of even more new stout ones the following spring.

Once the hedge has achieved the height and bulk you desire, each winter, when you can see what you are doing, you can start taking out, at ground level, one or two of the older shoots that will have become woody and less productive. You can even prune the whole hedge down by about half if it threatens to grow too tall. You can be quite tough with Rugosas, as they will produce flowers from new growth as well as old. Some varieties are leggier than others and how much maintenance you eventually do depends on what kind you have planted. You'll quickly get the hang of things once you understand how they work.

A STRIPPER AND BLACK TIGHTS

In the spirit of using what you have to hand rather than investing in expensive equipment, Willem from Horndean in Hampshire writes to say that he uses a wallpaper stripper to sterilise small quantities of home-made compost. He points out that the steamer fits snugly over seed trays and can be used prior to seed sowing.

I also had some interesting correspondence on the subject of uses for old tights in the garden—where would we gardeners be without them? Margaret from Gloucestershire lines the bottom of plant pots with cut-off bits of them to keep out ants. Jenny uses twisted sections of dark brown ones as tree ties. Sometimes the squirrels steal them, she says... The mind boggles. I stuff sections of old black ones tightly with barley straw and put them in my pond (barley straw helps control blanket weed as it rots down).

Another Margaret puts llama poo into an old leg and dangles it in a butt of water to produce a potent fertiliser. In the absence of llamas, horse or goat would do as well, she assures me. Madeleine from Christchurch and Gwen from Colchester find that the feet of old tights make excellent, easy-to-clean strainers when fastened around the downpipes that feed their water butts. Marion uses them for storing and hanging up her onions. I bet that looks wild.

An email from Polly informs us that her grandfather used to use a section of his wife's stockings to enclose his cabbages and cauliflowers to keep the leaves tightly closed (and presumably this also helped to protect them from caterpillar infestation). She has herself used the legs of tights to transport bunches of long-stemmed flowers in the car that would have otherwise got damaged. She wraps the cut stems in damp newspaper first.

Deryn from Sanderstead and Susan from Bury St Edmunds both use the ends of tights as hammock-style supports for ripening melons, tying the ends to canes. The give in the material allows for the growth of the fruit. Meanwhile Mary snips bits from her old tights and slips them over ripening bunches of cherries to keep the birds off them.

Anne from Eastbourne and emailer Helen both turn bits of old brown tights into discreet, stretchy plant ties, while Janet hangs small bundles of cut hair (from her hairdresser's floor, presumably) stuffed into sections of old tights, in amongst the branches of her shrub roses to put off nibbling deer.

Jane of Yateley in Hampshire puts her pond pump inside the knotted- up top section of a pair of tights to stop it getting clogged with sludge and creepy crawlies. The makeshift pump cover is easily removed, rinsed and replaced. And finally, Joy from Torpoint in Cornwall stores old plastic plant pots in the legs of old tights, which stops them from toppling over on to the floor of her shed.

FLEA BEETLES

The white spots on Alexander's wild rocket are the work of tiny, black, extremely determined flea beetles. He could try creeping up on the plants armed with a piece of card painted with glue of some sort, and pass the card swiftly over them, a few inches above. The beetles will hop upwards and get stuck in the glue—in theory. The rocket with its little perforations will still be edible, so I suppose Alexander's other option is to just learn to eat rocket with his eyes tightly closed. Needless to say, neither of these slightly dippy activities should be witnessed by friends or neighbours.

SPORTS AND SUCKERS

Rodney from Retford has a flourishing white rose, 'Winchester Cathedral', that has this year for the first time produced one rogue stem of lovely, flattish pink roses. Is this an unusual phenomenon, he asks?

Apparently this kind of behaviour is not uncommon amongst roses that originated from 'sports' of others. In this case, your rose has reverted to 'Mary Rose' from whence 'Winchester Cathedral' originally came. The 'rogue shoot' can be cut right out, but if left it will not take over the bush, as if it were a sucker (a shoot produced from below a graft that grows from the vigorous root of a wild rose on to which some roses are grafted).

Which brings me briefly to the subject of identifying rose suckers. Peter from Scunthorpe wants to know how you can tell suckers from 'the real thing', and what you should do about them. Rose suckers have paler, matter green leaves than the roses from which they shoot, and they generally come up out of the soil a few inches from its main stem. You should grub around, find where they connect to the root, and rip them off (taking care not to de-stabilise the entire bush). If you simply prune them above ground level you will get two suckers instead of one.

MOVING A RHODODENDRON

I have a largish rhododendron that I need to move because of a small house extension. It is about 6ft (1.8m) high and the same in diameter. It has finished flowering for this year and the blooms are now dying off. I would like to transplant it but have no idea how to do this without killing it in the process. Can you advise please?
Peter, Chichester

It would seem to be a little-known fact that you can do quite unspeakably brutal things to rhododendrons and they will almost always (I feel duty bound to include here an uncharacteristic note of hedge-betting) come back smiling. Early in my gardening career I watched, amazed, while an uncle of mine whose Buckinghamshire garden included a lush little piece of birch woodland positively littered with camellias, rhodies and all manner of woodlanders, dug up a large specimen, barrowed it to another part of the wood and dug it in amid tons of natural leaf litter—in mid-summer. I have ever since been a courageous—you might say foolhardy—transplanter, and got away with an awful lot.

The secret, with rhododendrons, lies in the fact that they have compact and relatively shallow root systems. You should drip a hose into the base of the plant overnight (or, even better, water thoroughly and slowly with rainwater) before you try to dig it up. Do this based on an estimate that the roots' spread will be around half the spread of its branches, and that they will go down about 18in (45cm). Prepare the plant's new site before you dig it up, based on the above dimensions plus a bit extra and incorporate leaf mould or ericaceous compost into the soil as you dig it over. Soak this prepared planting hole well. Since your rhododendron is a considerable size, you would do well to prune it down a bit to make it more manageable. Fear not though, it will shoot out from naked woody stems if needs be, although it will not flower on its new growth next year. It will of course be tremendously heavy—a thick plastic sheet that you can drag may be more helpful than a barrow. When you have manhandled the plant into its new home and firmed it well in, water it again and mulch it heavily with something comforting. Last year's half-rotted leaf mould would be perfect.

IN DEFENCE OF JUST MOWING

As a nation, we gave up wearing socks with sandals and started lunching outdoors 35 years ago—coinciding, I remember, with a couple of arid summers when even the most meticulous gardeners were forced to sit by while their lawns went brown and scrunchy. Subsequently the socks stayed off (thank goodness) and we kept our taste for 'alfresco dining' (what a loathsome cliché that has become), but have rapidly returned to our masochistic habit of fiddling around endlessly and spending a small fortune in pursuit of the perfect lawn.

Most of us—and I definitely include myself here—still hanker after a bit of lawn to sit on. Attempts to woo us with other fads have been partially successful. But wild flower meadows are not in the least labour saving, ditto prairie planting, which anyway is a mite too 'foreign' for most British tastes. So despite my acknowledged lack of perfectionism I make considerable efforts in order to keep the green bits of the garden looking good, and I actually find mowing rather therapeutic. But I hesitate to write about my 'lawn'. I never attempt to kill the moss, which in winter and early spring is almost overwhelming, I never apply fertiliser and never water, and I only ever spot weed the real bad boys—thistles and dandelions—the weeds that would certainly mark me as a Really Bad Gardener. Shock horror.

From April to October I mow weekly, using a rotary mower with the blade set, in high summer, on the lowest setting that I can get away with. Edging shears are regularly used with precision to get the desired manicured effect. I now definitely have the upper hand, and can claim to have a tolerably neat greensward except during drought—and even after this it never fails to revive. True, I can't cut my 'lawn' as short as perfectionists would like, and from time to time it sports extraordinarily pretty outbreaks of flowers, the ground-hugging 'weeds' that lie down under the mower—heavenly blue-eyed speedwell, self-heal, clover and buttercup. But, I ask, is that really so terrible?

August

THE GRASS IS ALWAYS GREENER...
WHEN YOU GET HOME

It is that time of year again. The keenest among us may find themselves somewhat reluctantly shoehorning themselves and their families into airline seats or nose-to-tailing it in motorway queues, wondering what kind of horticultural wreck they will find when they return. It does seem slightly crazy, somehow, to abandon garden and greenhouse when they are at their best—and most needy of our attention. There are some steps you can take to alleviate the anxiety and make it easier to knock things back into shape more quickly after a holiday. But of course it does mean a bit of forethought and extra gardening before you leave.

Shrubs. Make sure that you have cut back and fed those that have already finished flowering. This will include the philadelphus, weigelas, and evergreens such as ceanothus and *Viburnum tinus*. Foliage evergreens such as pittosporums should be thinned out or cut back if appropriate. Privet hedges that grow really fast can be left, but should be a priority job when you get home, since a freshly cut hedge (along with a newly mown lawn) will instantly tart up even the most lacklustre of late summer gardens. If all of this is out of the question, at the very least deadhead the roses.

Flowers. Try to find time to also deadhead the entire herbaceous population before you leave. The really strong-willed can go even further, and remove soon-to-open buds as well, on the grounds

125

that it will take two weeks for the plants to make new ones that will open in time to welcome them home. Cut the old flower stems of lupins and delphiniums right down to ground level and give them a liquid feed to encourage a second flush later, and take the shears to—or at least cut or tug out the outermost lolling spent flower stems—of those herbaceous plants that are just past their best, such as catmint, alchemilla and border geraniums.

Boring jobs. Those that we put off because they take time to bear fruit can be tackled just before you leave. Rough up the soil on bare patches of lawn and re-seed them, mixing the seed with potting compost and tamping it all down lightly before covering it with chicken wire. Take the opportunity to apply glyphosate weedkiller to bindweed stems, having carefully disentangled them from host plants and shoved the stems in a plastic bag. When you return the grass will have germinated and the weedkiller will have done its job.

Grass. The thing that shocks us the most when we get home is the sky-high grass. If you are going away for more than two weeks, if at all possible get someone to mow it for you at least once. Even a botched job by a reluctant juvenile will be better than nothing. When you return, do not mow on the lowest setting for a week or two. But really, the lawn should be the least of your worries. Grass absolutely always recovers.

Watering. Make life easier for those left in charge by grouping houseplants together in the bath or by the kitchen sink. Separate out the succulents and any that can cope for the duration

126

without water and put them elsewhere, or they may drown. Outside, move smaller pots into the shade—even real sun-lovers will be fine for a couple of weeks. Soak any vulnerable newly planted treasures deeply before you go and just keep your fingers crossed—you can't really expect anyone to water your borders. Remember that no one knows or cares about your garden like you do. Holidays are much easier in February.

HOLIDAY SEEDS

A word about Holiday Seeds—those strange unidentifiable seedpods and fruit stones that make their way back to this country from all points of the globe in your pockets and spongebags. If you try to germinate them, see it as a bit of an adventure. You may get temporary, lanky houseplants out of them. But mangoes in Maidstone and avocados in Accrington? I think not.

Although I have had an email from Sheila who has managed to grow a proper, sweet and juicy pineapple in Surrey—from the sprouted top of a supermarket fruit nurtured on the south-east-facing windowsill of her office. Further north, Trevor has got four small paw-paw trees growing from seed in his garden in Shropshire. He is wisely going to put one in the greenhouse for the winter.

DEUTZIA DILEMMA

Jane has got in a pickle with a summer pruning job and needs some advice. The problem is an inherited large white double-flowered deutzia (probably *Deutzia scabra* 'Candidissima'), which flowered badly this year and currently consists of 9ft (2.7m) of woody bare stems with a tuft of leaves on top. She has had conflicting advice: books tell her to cut some of the old shoots down to the ground, while a friend urges her to cut the whole thing right down.

The difficulty with large deutzias, and with those other old grand duchesses, weigela (to which deutzias are related) and philadelphus is that they are not particularly lovely things except when they are in flower. Certainly in small garden settings they need careful management, and should ideally not be planted where they can't be easily reached. Sensitive pruning at the right time (immediately after flowering, inconveniently bang in the middle of the best bit of summer), enables them to melt into the surrounding greenery once they have done their glorious stuff and while they get on with producing the new shoots that will flower the following year.

Of course Jane could leave her deutzia until next July before carrying out what I call 'first-aid pruning', but I suspect she rather wants to get on with it now, even though it is rather late in the season. I think she should follow her friends' advice and cut the whole thing down to about 3ft (1m). Any new shoots trying to grow from below this point should be preserved if possible, and any dead and ancient wood removed completely. A slim pruning saw (as made by Wilkinson) will probably be a vital tool for this job. The compacted soil around the base of the shrub should be carefully loosened, a couple of fistfuls of general fertiliser sprinkled round, two large cans of water slowly applied and a thick comforting mulch (compost, leaf mould) applied all around. With any luck the shrub, even at this stage of summer, will produce some new, straight young shoots from the newly cut 'crown' and even one or two from ground level. It may well flower on some, if not all, of these next year, and the shrub will look a lot better.

Once renovated in this way, subsequent pruning should be relatively easy—the cutting back of all shoots that have flowered, some of them right down to just above the woody crown that was created by the 'first aid pruning', some of them half way, while every year or two removing something old from the bottom.

By the way, for those who never dared ask... Deutzia should be pronounced doyts-e-a.

There is a wonderful little paperback *Plant Names Simplified* by A T Johnson and H A Smith that helps with difficult pronunciation. Fascinating bedtime browsing.

SHRUBS FROM SEEDS?

An email from Nicole asks, is it worth potting up some of the myriad seedlings of shrubs that seem to grow easily in the gravel at the edge of her drive? Will they take years to do anything?

I have to admit to rather enjoying this kind of informal, hit and miss plant production myself, and generally have a few junior home-grown hebes or phlomis plants lurking around in pots in my rudimentary nursery area, together with *Leycesteria formosa* seedlings 'sown' indiscriminately for me by birds and subsequently potted up. My particular offspring of this quick-growing shrub seem to have eye-catchingly dark flowers and berries.

So my answer to the first part of Nicole's question is 'yes', it is worth it, if you have the space, time and, most of all, the inclination to look after little 'free' plants. Generally it is easy to identify broadly what you have by looking at the young foliage, but it is quite fun to see what variations and surprises turn up. The seedlings are vulnerable in infancy, as you transfer them from where they naturally wanted to grow into pots of sandy compost, but they soon perk up and take off.

As to the second part of the question: it is also 'yes'. These plants may take a year or two to flower, perhaps more, by which time they will need to have been potted on, working their way up through the John Innes soil-based composts until they end up in 2-litre pots of good, gutsy J I No 3, with a little added leaf mould or home-made compost to lighten it up a bit. You could take the whole thing quite seriously and designate a small area of your garden to them, sinking the pots in the soil to make sure they keep cool and watering them consistently, feeding them with a liquid feed occasionally when they are in growth. Pinching out the growing tips of any that grow lanky after their first year will make them bush up into substantial, manageable little plants. Once the little shrubs are more or less mature, you will be able to see which ones have come 'true' and which, if any, are interesting oddities that are worth nurturing further.

BETTERING ONE'S HEDGES

Emailer Paul wants to know what he can do to improve/thicken up a thin and wispy old *Lonicera nitida* hedge that suffered for years from too little light under a shade-casting tree that has now been removed. Drastic action might be the best way forward here. Lonicera will grow back extremely quickly even if it is cut to the quick—and major surgery will give the opportunity to loosen the soil gently around the base of the hedge and feed it with a general fertiliser as well, to speed recovery. Once it has become substantial again, the renovated hedge will need trimming lightly twice each summer to encourage thick, bushy growth.

A gardening couple near Leatherhead, Surrey, have a rather complicated hedge problem of a different kind. For five years or more *She* has argued that a tall internal beech hedge should be removed to reveal a much better view of nearby rolling countryside (including their own field). Meanwhile *He* resists all pressure to change the garden so completely. It was ever thus. In a gardening partnership there is often one who cannot visualise the outcome of major works, and one for whom this provides a constant source of frustration. Might I suggest a compromise? Reduce a section to 18in (45cm) as a taster for things (hopefully) to come. If *He* is unable to cope with the whole dramatic removal, let it grow back (it will take about two years at most). Hopefully, once *He* can actually see the potential improvement, the decision to remove the hedge won't be so difficult.

131

SHADY STUFF

Pete from County Wicklow, who clearly has a problem getting things going in shade, asks me for a list of appropriate herbaceous plants. My first thought? What kind of shade is he struggling with? There is shade that is a result of overhanging deciduous trees, there is shade—generally for only part of the day—that is the result of nearby tall walls or (even worse) mammoth hedges, and there is deep inhospitable shade to be found under the canopy of wide-spreading evergreens such as yew.

The first is relatively easy to deal with since at least the area will receive light and rain during the winter and spring. A simple but limited solution would be to take inspiration from our woodland margins, mulch with composted bark and leaf mould and nurture native bluebells, wood anemones, primroses and campion, writing the area off for the later part of the year when the tree canopies thicken. This is clearly more appropriate in larger gardens. On a smaller scale you could dress things up a bit with more 'garden-y' planting: for example, hellebores, snowdrops, some of the sprawly shade-tolerant geraniums, such as *Geranium phaeum* and *G. macrorrhizum,* and a mass of variegated white honesty, which is surprisingly lovely in dappled shade. Tiny cyclamen will colonise freely and extend the season of interest.

The problem of planting under the canopy of yew trees and other dense evergreen trees is pretty much insurmountable. In an area in my garden that is similarly afflicted, I have got round it by using planters and it is now home to a successful

132

cacophony of loud, shapely things in large pots and urns, including box balls, a thriving tree fern, *Melianthus major*, hostas and various spiky things—carefully grouped and watered and groomed when necessary. The whole thing is rather eye-catching and solves the problem nicely.

Which brings me to the most common shade quandary—namely, how do you create a decent northish-facing border that is dominated by the shade cast by a tall wall or hedge? Even if the area gets blistering sun for a few hours each day in summer, you will get on much better if you abandon all thoughts of sunny things and plant it up purely with shade-lovers. Many perennials will put on a decent show as long as (and this is the absolute key to success) you improve the soil with plenty of moisture-retaining stuff—garden compost, composted bark and leaf mould, for example—and mulch after planting. If there is space to do so, leave a no-man's land path at the back between the wall or hedge, since the soil is likely to be rotten and/or root infested and impossibly dry there anyway. This will also bring the border forward a little out of the gloom. The list of herbaceous plants that will work here is huge. Some of my favourites are *Astrantia major* and the less well-known *Silene fimbriata* (a frilly petalled white campion), *Lamium orvala* (a tall, dusky-pink dead nettle), *Gillenia trifoliata*, *Kirengeshoma palmata*, *Lunaria rediviva* (the pretty, lilac-flowered perennial honesty), as well as *Euphorbia amygdaloides*, Japanese anemones, hostas, ferns, lily-of-the-valley and of course the geraniums and woodlanders mentioned above.

MUDDY GRASS UNDER PERGOLA

The grass on our 6ft (1.8m) wide path dies where it passes under a 12ft (3.6m) long pergola which has, over the years, formed a dark tunnel, densely planted with honeysuckle and jasmine. Is there any kind of grass seed that we can sow that will cope with this situation?
Jonathan, by email

The conditions you describe are about the most difficult imaginable for grass growth. Although 'shade-tolerant' grass seed is readily available and would germinate well in spring and grow for a few weeks before the foliage on the pergola thickened up, it is really only successful in light, dappled shade. Dense shade during the summer, coupled with inevitable lack of moisture and, since this is a pathway, presumably a considerable amount of foot traffic, are bound to take their toll. For practical and aesthetic reasons, I would abandon grass altogether in this area, and either brick or pave it. Alternatively you could use wide slabs of York paving or one of the excellent mellow-looking fakes as stepping-stones through the 'tunnel'. The space in between the stepping-stones could be covered in medium-grade bark chippings, which would look a lot better than compacted soil and the spindly remnants of grass. In autumn, the fallen leaves would not need to be swept, but would quickly be absorbed into the bark.

Some years ago I visited a garden where the owner made quite a feature of a leafy tunnel like yours, and furnished it with a weathered statue (of Pan, I think), with a froth of variegated ivy around its feet. It was simple and really charming—silk purses, sows' ears and all that.

RAMBLING ON AND ON

Having mismanaged a rambler rose on a 30ft (9m) pergola for several years—pruning it in winter assuming it was a climber and thus removing most of its flowering shoots—I finally got it right (following your instructions) and it is now a mass of flowers in late June. However, the new shoots produced at this time of year are quite overwhelming and I fear they will destroy the pergola. Should I cut out some of the new stout growth now, as well as trying to get some of the old flowering shoots out?
Margaret, Godalming, Surry

It sounds to me as if this is one of those mighty 'wild' ramblers. The most notorious of these is *Rosa filipes* 'Kiftsgate', the very name of which can strike fear into the hearts of gardeners everywhere who have had their fingers burnt—or should that be pricked? These enormous roses really need to find their way into big old trees where they can be left well alone.

Yes, you should remove a lot of the new 'powershoots' that threaten to overwhelm the pergola and cut out such ex-flowering shoots as you can easily reach. Cover your arms or wear a wax jacket for protection. Once growth has stopped in December, get in amongst the beast again, remove more of the old growth and even more of lengthy newer growth, cutting off the tips of shoots that are over-long and tying in just enough of what is left to provide a good show of flowers next year.

A warning to all new gardeners—these gorgeous roses are not for the faint-hearted, or for small gardens.

KNAUTIA WITH MILDEW

We have a **Knautia macedonica** *that usually flowers non-stop. This year it is covered in powdery mildew. I know that this is due to dry conditions and bad air circulation, but do you think it would be worth cutting it back or is it too late to do this? If cutting back is a good idea, how far should I go?*
Monica, by email

This is a problem I know well. Knautia is a favourite border plant of mine with its deep, dark crimson pincushion flowers. It is, as you so rightly say, a reliable non-stop flowerer and unless fanatically deadheaded, it self-seeds into the bargain. You are right in your diagnosis of mildew and its causes and in your instinct to cut it right back—you certainly have nothing to lose by doing so, and the plant may well rally and produce fresh flowering growth within a couple of weeks that is 'cleaner' than the dusty-looking grey mess that currently adorns it. Cut away all of the nasty foliage and you will very probably find tiny leaves already struggling through beneath it. Water well (use a soluble fertiliser if you are so inclined) and mulch the soil around its base. You could try using a systemic fungicide on the new growth when it starts to plump up and this may stave off a recurrence of the disease, particularly if the weather becomes hot and dry again.

DEADHEADING ROSES

I have been told that the accepted way to deadhead a rose is simply to pinch off the head—or is this just pub talk? My wife taught me to cut the stem to a strong outward-growing bud to help ensure repeat flowering and a compact bush.
Tony, Bourne End, Buckinghamshire

I am sure you don't need me to tell you that your wife is right. Using secateurs, you should snip off the old flower head or heads with about 6in (15cm) of stem, including two or three leaves, cutting at a point just above a leaf on the outside of the bush. From the base of that leaf the next flower shoot should appear.

And yet... and yet... What should you do about the old Floribundas and some of the modern roses, many of which (like my wonderful 'Bonica') produce a succession of flowers over a period of three weeks or more from huge congested trusses? It is for these that the old finger and thumb routine is useful. As each flower fades you can manually tweak or scissor-snip out each one, or just shake the cluster or fiddle off the old petals with your fingers—anything to make the truss look neater and prevent wet weather from sticking everything together into a mouldering mass and ruining the remaining flowers before their time. Once 80 per cent of the little flowers have had their day, you can do the 'right' thing and cut the whole stem down, in the approved manner.

It goes without saying that only dead heads would deadhead species roses such as *Rosa glauca* or *R. moyesii*, which have good hips. But I will say it anyway.

MITEY PROBLEMS

Every year my **Crocosmia** *'Lucifer' ends the season disastrously, with spider mite. I cut my plants down as soon as I realised they had a problem, and now find that other plants are being attacked. Should I throw away the infected corms? What spray can I use to control or eradicate the spider mite on other plants? Should I spray the fence and soil as well? My garden is tiny.*
Meredy, London

As a former London gardener, I utterly sympathise: this can be a serious problem in hot little urban courtyard gardens. Glasshouse red spider mite, as it is called, is

138

seen by many experts as purely a greenhouse/indoor problem, and much of the advice you can glean from books concentrates on biological control using a predatory species of mite, *Phytoseiulus*, which of course is useless outdoors.

Perhaps I should here describe the spider mite 'symptoms' for the benefit of the uninitiated. Almost invisible to the naked eye, spider mites colonise the backs of leaves of various ornamental plants (crocosmia and herbaceous geraniums are favourite haunts), which gradually go dry, brown and curl up— bang in the middle of summer. Only when the infestation is advanced can you sometimes see the mites shinning up and down the very fine webbing that they construct within the curled leaves. They multiply rapidly during hot dry weather between June and September and can travel from plant to plant, even creating a visible beige 'track' across the garden, often in the direction of the prevailing draughts.

The best defence is to plant less intensively (some hope, in a tiny garden...) and to mist foliage regularly in the evening to cut down their breeding rate (not easy if there is a hosepipe ban). As you have done, you should always cut off and burn or destroy infected foliage, but the destruction of the corms may not be necessary—give them another year. In winter the females turn red and hibernate in clusters in nooks and crannies in fences and walls so are relatively easy to spot. I would have a go at seeking them out before they re-emerge next year and scrub/spray suspect areas in winter with a garden cleaning agent such as Jeyes Fluid (avoiding foliage). Although spider mite is not listed as one of its target nasties, you could try spraying with imidacloprid (such as Provado Ultimate Bug Killer) in May or early June.

GONE TO SEED

As a relatively new gardener I don't know whether the green seed pods need to be left on the plant until they dry out, or if they can be picked to tidy up the garden and dried indoors.
Rosemary, by email

Since you say you are a relatively new gardener I make no apologies for the following extremely basic information that I feel may be of help.

Almost before the seedpods have a chance to form on your fading summer flowers, you can remove them, along with a short piece of the stem, generally cutting just above a leaf joint where a new tiny shoot or flower bud may be already discernible. This tidying up exercise (deadheading) becomes a useful routine, the wonderful by-product being that it will prolong the flowering season of most (but not all) of your summer flowers. The reason for this is that once plants have set seed, their flowering slows down and eventually stops—their reproductive work is done for the year. So by deadheading regularly you can, as it were, fool them into

140

thinking they need to go on flowering. Only if the seed heads themselves are intrinsically beautiful or if you want to save seed (for yourself or for garden birds to feast on) do you leave the pods to mature and ripen on the plant. If you do want to save seed, you harvest the pods just before they have a chance to cast their contents around, as they are meant to do. With some plants you can deadhead for a few weeks, eventually leaving the last lot of flowers to make seed in early autumn, which you can then save.

Seed heads plucked off the plant when they are still green seldom contain seed that is viable—which is why garden owners regard it as such a dastardly act when visitors to their gardens surreptitiously try a little impromptu, premature 'deadheading' on the sly.

HYDRANGEA COLOUR…

Lesley has had trouble taking cuttings of various strongly coloured hydrangeas. Her cuttings always turn out to have washy pink flowers, and she wonders if this always happens. Now living in West Yorkshire (with very acid soil) she has tried again—taking cuttings from her neighbour's very beautiful deep blue-flowered bush. She has planted them in pots of a mixture of garden soil and compost, and yet again they have flowered pink. I suspect it is the combination of the compost mixture together with limey tap water with which she must be watering them that is turning them pink. If she gets the plants into the ground with the truly acid local soil like her neighbour's, they

141

should revert to their lovely blue. This is borne out by the fact that the neighbour successfully propagates the bush normally by layering (pegging shoots down to the soil to encourage them to root naturally while still attached to the 'mother' plant). Pink hydrangeas can, of course, be persuaded to go blue by being treated with hydrangea colourant (which changes the soil pH) that can be bought from nurseries.

...DRYING HYDRANGEAS

Frances asks if I could write a little about cutting hydrangeas for dried flowers. When is the best time to cut them, and are there any tips I can give to make sure they retain their colours? I have to say that I do not cut my own hydrangea flower heads but leave them to go brown on the shoot tips for the winter to protect the delicate buds from frost. However I have a sister-in-law with a mild gulf-stream garden in western Scotland, full of scores of beautiful hydrangeas which she cuts by the armful, dries and gives away to friends—so I asked her. She cuts them just as they are about to 'go over' and starting to feel slightly papery—but before they show any hint of browning. She then stands them in waste-paper baskets, loosely 'arranged' so that the air can circulate freely, overnight on top of the Aga lid. Or she ties the heads together in pairs and hooks them over an old ceiling-mounted airing rack. The quicker they dry and the less they touch each other, the better. Some varieties keep their colour better than others, she said—but since she has no idea what hers are called, she was not able to be more specific.

142

FINAL CUT FOR PRIVET

John gave a mighty overgrown privet hedge in his new garden a really severe haircut back in June, but thereafter it rather got away from him and he asks if it will do the hedge any harm if he has another go at it before the winter. Unless his hedge is grown in a really sheltered site, it will be dropping almost all of its leaves in the next few weeks and may look quite gaunt for the winter anyway. Privet is quite a tough old beast, and if he cuts it now it will just leaf up a little late next spring but should otherwise come to no harm. Privet virtually stops growing in late August, and I find that if I make time to cut it then (not the most pleasant task on a hot day), it looks immaculate until the following April—bar the odd whiskery bits that appear in early autumn and can just be lopped off with a pair of hand shears.

AGAPANTHUS

I am having problems with my potted agapanthus that isn't doing as well as it used to, and put on a poor show this summer. I have always understood that agapanthus appreciated being pot bound, fed and watered well, and needed full sun. Mine gets all this. Now I have read that it needs a long root run and plenty of space. Which is right?
Rosemary, Hammersmith, West London

This is one of those occasions where, in the face of conflicting opinions, I can only tell about my own experience, in the hope that it might be useful.

As far as I am concerned, potted agapanthus definitely deteriorate as they become truly pot bound, probably because it becomes increasingly difficult to feed and water them. I have to say that my most successful plants—hardier Headbourne hybrids—survived well outside in the ground (in south-east England) in an extremely well-drained situation that had sun all year round. I gave them a protective mulch in the autumn and fed them with a slow-release fertiliser in the spring and again just as they started flowering in late summer—they expanded and produced more flowers each year.

Plants of the stouter, altogether more dramatic and exotic, evegreen *Agapanthus africanus* are rather less hardy than the hybrids and definitely need to be grown in pots and given winter protection. The pots should be kept barely moist during the winter months. Every few years they should be re-potted, and can also be divided.

LAVENDER TRIMMING

My two-year-old Hidcote lavender hedge was just perfect this year. How do I stop it going downhill from here? I have received conflicting advice about pruning it. Once a year? Twice a year?
Miriam, Hertfordshire

I definitely belong in the twice-a-year camp. I presume that, like mine, your Hidcote lavender has just about finished flowering, although it may (tantalisingly but rather annoyingly, really) be still carrying just a few flowers. I always cut my earlyish flowering lavender such as this one twice, once in August—even though this means cutting off the stragglers—and again in late February. The first cut is surprisingly hard. I take the shears and trim it right back, removing the old flowers and their stalks, and another 2–3in (5–8cm) of foliage so that for a while the bushes look like little grey hedgehogs—just the lowest few pairs of tiny emerging whiskery grey shoots in evidence. The bushes then 'recover' during the next few weeks and become pleasing hummocks for the winter. Then in February (or March if the weather is revolting), I give the bushes a light trim all over and away they go. I find that two cuts a year keeps them admirably compact and dumpy, which for a lavender hedge is particularly important.

WHAT CANNA DO NEXT YEAR?

I bought four potted canna lilies in late April, already shooting and looking healthy. As advised I kept them in my unheated greenhouse until late May, when I transplanted them into large tubs outside. Two of them are now in flower and they are doing a splendid job of hiding my failed sweet peas. I have seen a great clump of cannas living rough outside. Should I plant mine out for next year?
Frances, by email

In my experience—and I live in the relatively mild south-east—cannas are barely hardy, which is unsurprising since many of them come originally from sub-tropical South America. I suspect that the ones that you have seen ' living rough' are in a really sheltered spot, are probably given a thick dry mulch (of straw or bracken, pegged down under fleece), or that the sheer size of the clump means that at least some of it may get frost protection from its own foliage as it dies down.

My advice would be to keep them in containers—the same ones, if you can shift them into an unheated greenhouse, porch or garage for the winter. Their compost should remain barely moist. Next spring simply replace the top few inches of compost with leaf mould or peat-free multi-purpose compost peppered with some slow-release fertiliser and keep them in a bright, warm place until May or June, by which time they will have good sturdy shoots. The following year you may need to un-pot them and divide them, but I would certainly always regard them as container plants.

OLEANDERS

I have three oleanders grown from cuttings, all of which develop buds but never fully bloom. A local garden centre advised a slow-release fertiliser but this has not overcome the problem.
Mike, *by email*

There is a dearth of information here, but I will make certain assumptions since this seems to be a common problem with oleanders grown out of their comfort zone in the UK—and therefore one definitely worth airing here.

I am assuming, for example, that these plants of *Nerium oleander*—to give them their 'proper' name—are in containers. Some gardeners in our most southerly counties seem to get away with growing oleanders in the ground outside and those who can offer them year-round sun and complete shelter from plunging winter temperatures and prolonged wet manage to get them to flower well, but it is not usual. My experience with oleanders is that even potted plants need quite careful management if they are to burst into flower in high summer. I overwinter mine in an (unheated) greenhouse from early October and for at least a month longer than you could possibly imagine they need: I don't

147

put them outside until well into June. Then I give them the warmest, sunniest spot I can find. At this point I cut off any stems with unopened flower buds on them that look even slightly dried up and tired (often cutting their stems right down to a point just above some newly emerging shoots—effectively pruning them). This still leaves a lot of growth with younger, fatter, more promising-looking flower buds. I find that then, provided we have a couple of weeks of good sunny weather, everything kicks off nicely.

Anything else? Oleanders seem to thrive in stony soil—try loam-based John Innes No 3. A high potash feed (tomato food, for example) is a good idea once they are brought outside for the summer, but rich sponge-y soil and lavish feeding does not seem to be necessary and could encourage floppy growth at the expense of flowers. And it is worth reminding readers that they are extremely poisonous.

PASSION FRUIT

My neighbour has planted a passion flower— but it is doing rather well on my side of the fence. We would both like to know if the fruits are edible, and if they are not, how safe are they for young children?
Veronica, by email

The fruits of the hardy passion flower, *Passiflora caerulea*, are quite safe for children. Though they are, shall we say, barely

148

palatable and somewhat tasteless, rather than edible, and are not the same variety as the sweeter black ones sold for eating, which are imported and come from the more tender *P. edulis*.

GROUND ELDER PLANTS FOR SALE

A garden-visiting companion expressed surprise and not a little horror when we saw variegated ground elder (*Aegopodium variegatum*, to honour it with a posh name) for sale in Beth Chatto's marvellous nursery. I confessed to her that I had just days before begged a trowel-full from another friend, who grows it in the dry, dimly lit gravel on the north-facing side of her house, where it does an admirable, controllable job. The same friend also keeps a really good-looking pot of it, tucked away in some impossibly deep shade under her trees—which is what I intend to do as well. This, then, is the secret of this would-be bogeyman: treat it (really) mean, keep it (fairly) lean.

WHAT TO DO WITH EARWIGS?

And finally a touch of savagery: June, as advised, catches earwigs by putting flowerpots upside down on sticks among her dahlias and stuffing them with straw. What happens then? Nobody actually tells you, she says. There is an answer. Always use terracotta pots (rather than plastic) and (ahem... sorry, all you sensitive souls) simply set fire to the contents.

149

Autumn

September

COLOUR—IT'S NOT A BLACK AND WHITE ISSUE

As a child, art lessons were for me a chance to muck about and the nearest I came to colour appreciation was during school's dullest moments, when I would while away the time organising my treasured Derwent coloured crayons. Totally absorbed, I would start randomly and work my way through the entire collection (there were dozens of them), precisely graduating the colours so that through half-closed eyes they formed a gorgeous mesmerising blur.

Nor when I started gardening did colour consciously enter the frame. My mother, a skilled plantswoman whose primary influence was the late Margery Fish, the then chatelaine of East Lambrook Manor, talked little about how she put her gloriously stuffed borders together. Adopting her attitudes, I took to gardening with great zeal in my early thirties. While she and I talked basic plant physiology quite a bit (she was a botanist and a teacher by training), the use of colour and texture were never discussed. I put plants together in ways that worked for me, but I had no colour prejudices or strong preferences, nor a yen for colour-themed borders or anything regarded as remotely sophisticated. I was encouraged to enrich the soil, understand the needs of my plants—sun and drainage for this, shade and moisture for that—learn how to prune and so on, and just go

153

for it.

My first sight of a colour wheel in a fashionable coffee-table gardening book filled me with terror. There were, it transpired, 'rules' about complementary and harmonious colours that you were supposed to follow. Gardening acquaintances, presumed to be 'in the know', would discuss Gertrude Jekyll in hallowed tones and I would overhear dismissive conversations about certain colours (usually yellow or orange) or combinations of colours that were clearly, among those with 'taste', not tolerated.

Through those dark days of deeply silly insecurity, I kept my head down and through the usual combination of gardener's luck, trial and error, continued to learn. But I have since contracted a serious disease myself: I have caught colour. I think it probably happened a decade or so ago when I first visited Hadspen Garden in Somerset—then a mind-boggling place of magical colour and unfussy maintenance put together by Nori and Sandra Pope, who think, speak and write about colour in musical terms.

In the former vegetable garden of Hadspen House, they created a colour border stacked (for want of a better word) against a tall semi-circular brick wall several hundred feet long. Entering this area of the garden at the hot, south-facing end of the wall you were pitched straight into an ocean of plants with bleached cream and lemon flowers. Ahead the land dropped away to a totally yellow, lime and cream double border, feet high. Turning left, as the wall curved away, the colour in the flowers and foliage changed, a semi-tone at a time, through yellow, orange, vermilion and crimson

154

pinks to a crescendo of flowers and foliage of the deepest red, with which the name 'Hadspen' became synonymous. Then the increasingly shady border faded gorgeously back again. Certain plants were repeated but, with new companions, looked quite different.

Musical analogies were tempting—colour and texture here formed an intricate, sumptuous composition. Once your eyes tuned in, you saw connections everywhere between the foliage of this plant, the petals of another and the central stamens, stems or leaf backs of more. You saw 'hidden' colour in a plant that you associated with another—as in the glowing orange eyelet of a dark purple buddleja.

So which is more important, the art or the science of gardening? The way I put plants together changed completely—and for the better, I am sure—since I started to consider and understand colour and texture in plants. But on reflection, I am glad that I learnt how to grow things first, before I ever clapped eyes on Hadspen. For I am sure my gardening would have been a far more frustrating and hit and miss affair had I not.

(The great colour border at Hadspen is, alas, no more. The lessons learned by a whole generation of gardeners will never be forgotten, I am sure.)

GROUND ELDER CLEAN-UP

This can be a depressing time of year for perennial weed-warriors like Fiona. She has been putting up a good fight against ground elder (see also May, page 58) in a flowerbed that is home to some well-

155

established and much-loved perennials. As the foliage of the perennials is beginning to sag, she can see that this awful weed is still lurking in the centre of the clumps, ready to have another go next year. What, if anything, can she do to get rid of this pain-in-the-neck once and for all, she asks?

Unless you are prepared to seek out every ground elder leaf, every bindweed tendril, from the core of wanted plants and painstakingly paint them with glyphosate during the height of the growing season, you simply have to dig out the infested plants, meticulously remove the roots of the weeds (which are white and brittle, but can be carefully pulled out backwards from the underside of each root ball), 'clean up' the entire area and not replant until the coast is absolutely clear.

There is a positive side to all this. Fiona's well-established perennials could probably do with a bit of 'renovation' anyway. She should dig them up and split them, discarding the centres (the exhausted part) and retain two or three good pieces of each clump, shaking or washing off the old soil to make complete removal of weed roots easier. Then she should pot each section on into large black plastic pots (in which they will live for a whole growing season) using 3 parts John Innes compost to 1 part leaf mould or peat-free multi-purpose compost (to aid water retention), rather than garden soil.

Fiona should then fork the entire bed over, adding a couple of buckets of organic matter and a handful of bonemeal per square yard, keeping her eyes peeled for stray scraps of weed root. Next, the bed should be covered with a 3in (8cm) layer of composted bark or leaf mould (this bit is optional, but ground elder roots are persistent but shallow, and any missed scraps will snuggle upwards into the mulch and be easier to winkle out when they start to grow and show next spring). The black-potted plants can be put back on the bed, pushed down into the mulch a little. They will of course, need watering, but at least they will all be conveniently in one place, and their contents will expand into the good weed-free soil in the pots and double in size. Meanwhile, she could jolly up the area and hide the pots to some extent with some tall annuals (tobacco plants?) next summer; any persistent bits of weed remaining in the bed can easily be removed, either by forking or by carefully targeted spraying. Early next autumn, Fiona can ditch the annuals and (making sure that the potted plants themselves are 'clean') put everything back together again.

WHY THIS IS NOT A HACKING TIME OF YEAR

For scrupulously tidy gardeners we are entering a distressing season. All that saggy stuff in the borders, lawns covered in worm casts, rambling roses putting out yards of prickly shoots in all directions, forsythias and other floppy things growing out over the paths, grass too damp to mow and leaves, leaves, leaves, falling everywhere. Tut, tut and triple tut.

The frequent response of gardeners who cannot tolerate this inevitable all-pervading autumnal disorder tends, unfortunately, to consist of carrying out the Big Tidy-Up. While sorting out the shed, top-dressing the lawn, cleaning out the inside of the greenhouse before winter, building a new leaf heap are all honourable, thoroughly necessary autumn jobs for the obsessively neat amongst us, this is not a good time to wage war with loppers, pruning saws and secateurs unless you really know what you are doing. For the benefit of habitual hackers, I will explain why.

First, the roses. Those long, superfluous-looking shoots of ramblers and larger once-flowering shrub roses will carry the best of next year's flowers, so should not all be lopped off for the sake of neatness. Tie some in or just let them ramble up trees. If you must reduce the sheer volume of growth, cut out an older shoot from the bottom, which will bring down a substantial quantity of attached new growth as well, without overall damage to the remainder. The one or two vigorous shoots of true climbing roses should be bent gently into position now, to join in with the overall branch pattern. Other roses—the ordinary bushes that are probably still flowering—can be pruned properly in the new year, although in windy gardens the larger, more top-heavy varieties may need to have some top growth cut away carefully in order to minimise wind rock.

The flowering shrubs more or less divide themselves into two groups. The ones that have only just finished flowering—the buddlejas, hypericums and so on—should not be pruned hard until next March, especially the more tender ones such as ceratostigma, hydrangeas and various fuchsias, since the outer growth protects the emerging shoots beneath from winter frost.

The really vulnerable shrubs, at this time of

year, are the shrubs that flowered much earlier in the year and, since doing so, have produced masses of shoots that will flower well next spring. Unless they were pruned immediately after they flowered, they may have outgrown their position, produced flopping branches that block paths and doorways—looking, in fact, as though they are desperate for a short back and sides. In practical terms, obviously if things have got out of hand then excess growth must be removed. But, compulsive pruners, beware. If you take away all that verdant stuff, flowering may be pitiful next year. Each spring I get sad letters from people who went too far.

ACER IN A TIGHT (S)POT

I have a dark-leaved **Acer palmatum** *in a stoneware container about 1ft (30cm) square on my terrace. It is about 2ft 8in (80cm) high, and has not grown much in the five or six years that I have had it. It drops its leaves quite early in the autumn and does not seem very happy. I give it a little general-purpose fertiliser occasionally. I would appreciate your advice.*
V B, Hitchen, Hertfordshire

These Japanese acers are notoriously slow-growing—which is why, incidentally, they cost so much to buy. However I can't help feeling that the reason yours is particularly sluggish and unhappy—despite the occasional feeding—is due to the fact that it has been in the same pot for so long. I expect that the pot is now full of roots, dries out quickly and is

159

even difficult to water.

I suggest you get a larger container for it and replant it using ericaceous compost, which, being lime-free, the acer will appreciate. If the roots are completely congested you should try to tap some of the old soil off them and loosen them up a little, while trying not to damage them. Water the newly potted tree thoroughly to settle the soil, keep your fingers crossed and hope that it will leaf up when spring comes and improve next year. After so long in its old pot, this tree might find it difficult to produce the new roots that will stir it into action and allow it to grow.

If it does survive and thrive, you should re-pot it every two or three years and, in between times, replace the top few inches of compost each year, adding some slow-release fertiliser granules at the same time.

SQUIRRELS AND BULBS

Verity wonders how on earth squirrels know where bulbs are planted? Do they sit and watch us from the trees? I am told they can smell them, and when you plant bulbs, it helps if you clear up all the bits of dry bulb 'skin' that shed themselves around as you plant and dig the bulbs in more deeply than is generally recommended. Next year Verity could also try putting a layer of coarse chicken wire about 2in (5cm) down between the surface of the soil and the bulbs—squirrels don't like catching their fingernails in it, apparently, and give up.

160

IN PURSUIT OF WILD FLOWERS

I'd like to share a cautionary tale from my previous garden, where I had a small orchard. Said orchard, which could be glimpsed from the kitchen, became the subject of every clichéd fantasy imaginable: I pictured billowing white sheets on a sunny washing line slung between apple trees. I imagined sitting reading under the greengage tree amid gently swaying grasses surrounded by butterflies and lulled by the lazy creak-creaking of grasshoppers. I planted some rambler roses to wander up the trees, and waited to be transported to paradise.

I approached maintenance of this area with naïve optimism. Let it all go its own way for a year, and it will be abundant with flowers and teeming with wildlife. How wrong I was. It turned out that half of the orchard was stuffed with matronly yellow daffodils, while the few wild flowers that had survived the years of mowing—primroses and native bluebells—were confined to the bases of perimeter hedges. Only in the sub-soil thrown over an underground air raid shelter did wild flowers prosper in significant quantities: a carpet of blue speedwell materialised, followed by a spectacular mass of russet-orange-flowered *Hieracium* 'fox and cubs'. Elsewhere docks, thistles and hogweed appeared from nowhere, while the grass, much of it the dreaded Yorkshire fog, grew thigh high then fell over. By July it was an impenetrable wet thatch, the cutting of which took days and left mountains of uncompostable 'hay', stacked chaotically in all corners of the garden.

161

At the end of that first year, I was worn out and secretly alarmed about the amount of work the 'wild' garden created. One option was to weedkill, rotavate and replant with a wild flower/grass seed mixture that includes yellow rattle, a semi-parasitic plant that reduces the vigour of grass. But being short of essential resources—namely manpower, time and money—the simpler option seemed to be to embark on a programme of laborious mowing-and-picking-up that would get rid of some of the more overwhelming weeds and weed grasses, and reduce the overall lushness. I decided also to 'cheat' with a couple of packets of seeds.

First I removed about 5 sq yds (5 sq m) of turf from an area in the orchard that I could see from the house, lightly raked the soil and sprinkled it with a wild flower seed mix containing annuals such as poppies and corn cockle, together with easy perennials ox-eye daisy and campion. I loosely covered the patch with chicken wire and waited. The results in the first year were spectacular—and spectacularly artificial—as the whole patch became a blaze of picture-book colour. The following year the annuals were largely squeezed out, daisies and campion predominated and I moved some of these crowded, now well-established plants out to take their chances in the grass beyond. Then I thinned out the vigorous original 'nursery' every year, transplanting ever more plants into the grass around the orchard and beyond. These in turn self-seeded well in the carefully managed grass, which was quite beautiful once it was no longer so rampant, the various grass species creating a softly coloured tapestry of their own. Dock and thistles disappeared, while sorrel, hawkbit and knapweed regenerated spontaneously and the 'fox and cubs' scampered in all directions. All in all it was a success, once I'd worked out how to tackle it.

ROCK-HARD SOIL

The soil in emailer Beverly's garden is rock hard, she says—impossible to weed or even to put stakes in to support her plants and furthermore it has no worms in it. How best should she proceed?

This may be stating the obvious, but it is only sensible to try to weed clay soil like this after rain, unless you can fit a hoe in between your plants—in which case choose a hot day and dislodged weeds will wilt to death. However, in the longer term Beverly would do well to mulch beds and borders with compost twice a year, adding almost an equal quantity of grit as she does so, and fork it all in lightly, as best she can, between border plants when the soil is moist. No opportunity should be missed to add a mixture of grit (or horticultural sand) and compost to the soil—when replanting and transplanting, for example. Worms will always turn up naturally during the wet months (as lawn-people will testify). And worms seem delighted if you add organic matter to garden soil and will proceed to churn things helpfully around a bit. Over time, Beverly's topsoil will gradually improve and her gardening life will get easier.

DEALING WITH LIVERWORT

Can you please advise on the best method of getting rid of liverwort, which seems to be unaffected by glyphosate weedkillers such as Roundup.
Glynis, by email

Liverwort, that scaly green growth that develops on the soil surface, is a relation of moss, and is a symptom of shady, wet conditions where the soil is not disturbed by cultivation frequently enough. Glynis is right, weedkillers don't really touch it, and it can become a bit of an eyesore. The best thing to do is to scrape the layer of liverwort off the soil and bin it, then lightly fork over the soil underneath from time to time. The application of mulch to the problem area will make it less likely that moss or liverwort will get a firm foothold again. Liverwort is often present on the compost of plants bought from nurseries that have not re-potted them frequently enough. Look out, everyone, for the real Trojan horse: 'bargain' plants and old pots of things that have been dusted with a ½in (1cm) layer of new compost, under which a thick layer of liverwort lurks unseen... most probably with an invisible crop of hairy bittercress seeds that will germinate and proliferate as soon as you get home, just for good measure.

INVADING NETTLES

The selective weedkiller that I used to use to treat nettles in my garden (which is next to unkempt woodland) is no longer available. How should I control them? I am reluctant to blanket the whole area with a total weedkiller.
Stuart, by email

While I appreciate that you will always have a problem with nettles seeding themselves from the rough land next to yours, I am confident that you can control these nettles without resorting to wholesale chemical destruction. In my old garden I had, like you, a big battle to gain the upper hand, but I succeeded in about two seasons, mainly by rooting them out. Stinging-nettle roots, though extremely tough and fibrous, lie quite shallowly in the soil. I used to attack large patches by first cutting them down in the autumn. As soon as they made their presence felt again I used to fork out the worst of the very obvious, running yellow roots. If they broke off below the point at which they had visible, purplish growing points, they did not regenerate. Any I missed or could not shift with my fork, I allowed to grow until they were about 9in (23cm) high, and then I used a glyphosate weedkiller such as Roundup, carefully aiming it at just the shoot tips, using a cut-off plastic bottle as a directional cowl. Damage to neighbouring plants was absolutely minimal, and the nettles themselves started to yellow and distort (indicating that they were dying) within about a week. Once you have seen off the areas that have dense matted roots, maintaining control of young seedlings and runners invading from hedgerows is a relatively easy annual job.

LATE LILY BEETLES

I assumed I had got the upper hand with lily beetles earlier this year by using an insecticide, but was horrified to discover several adult beetles hiding on the undersides of the leaves when I was cutting down the stems of my lilies. Presumably I have caught (and squashed) these in the nick of time, but it got me wondering: where do lily beetles go in the winter when there is no 'food' for them?
Janet, Fordingbridge, Hampshire

Lily beetles, the scarlet-coated horrors that (with their equally destructive grubs) do so much damage to lilies and their close relations, actually hibernate in the top inch or two of soil, sometimes but not always, close to lilies themselves, and also in other undisturbed garden debris.

Their life cycle is worth knowing: surviving adults emerge from hibernation earlier than you might think and can most often be found enjoying an *hors d'oeuvre* of the new stems and foliage of fritillaries, for example, before moving on to their main meal—your lilies. If you spot them this early you can try, as the expression goes, to nip them in the bud.

166

Furthermore, forewarned is forearmed and it is worth making the effort to also protect the first new growth of your lilies with a carefully targeted systemic spray (such as Provado Ultimate Bug Killer), which will make them unpalatable. Unchecked, lily beetles couple somewhat frantically and lay eggs that you seldom see on the undersides of leaves. Dull orange grubs hatch out, cover themselves with vile excreta to deter predators and feast on the lily leaves and flowers, reducing them to rags. They pupate in the soil beneath the plants before hatching out in their scarlet livery—thus more than one generation is produced each year. Which is why it is important to check lily plants (as you did) late in the season, when the flowers have gone and you have rather taken your eye off the ball.

When disturbed, lily beetles always drop to the ground and lie motionless on their backs (thus becoming the very devil to spot). Defeating them without spraying involves a single-minded daily hunt for them and cannot, unlike many other small routine gardening jobs, be successfully accomplished with scissors, secateurs, a cup of coffee or something stronger in hand since it uses three of your four useful extremities. You need one hand to tap them off the plant, one hand to catch them (urgh) and one foot with which to stamp triumphantly.

A FIG DILEMMA

My fig tree, re-potted in the spring and roughly 3ft (1m) tall, has given about a dozen delicious ripe fruits this year. It has now thrown about 100 new baby figs. What should I do about them? My Italian neighbour who claims to be an expert says to remove them all. Is that right? Last year around 15 baby figs survived the hard winter and these are the fruits that developed.
Chris, Poole, Dorset

Your Italian neighbour is more or less right. In our climate those small, rock-hard figs that grow during the summer and look tantalisingly as though they might just become large enough and ripen before the temperatures dive, seldom survive the winter and should be removed, so that the tree can divert its energy into growing the figs that will reliably ripen next year—currently almost invisible little swellings in the axils of some of the leaves. Having said that, if your tree is extremely sheltered (and in Dorset, in a really sheltered spot in a pot, it may well be), you may be lucky, as you seem to have been last year. If I were you, in order to find out more, I would be tempted to leave just a handful of the little figs on your tiny tree to see what happens. But remove the other 90-odd.

PROBLEM SUCKERS

Two readers have problems with plant suckers: Jean's ornamental cherry is throwing up an alarming number of them. She cuts them out but this seems to make them worse. Is her tree about to die? Probably not—this is just the way with some cherries and cutting out the suckers does tend to make things worse, so I have no helpful advice to offer. Any attempt to poison the suckers may ultimately harm the parent tree to which they are attached. Mary, on the other hand, is suffering from a rash of suckers turning up in her lawn since she recently cut down and got rid of four stag's horn sumachs (*Rhus typhina*). If Mary can protect the grass around each sucker with plastic, while they are in leaf she could spray them with a heavy-duty weedkiller such as Tree Stump Killer (from Bayer), carefully following instructions on the pack.

A USE FOR OLD POTTING COMPOST

Each year when I plant out the pots in my garden I have a large amount of old potting compost. Is it possible in some way to reuse it by adding something to it so that I don't end up each year buying new compost?
Derek, Ferndown, Dorset

In theory you can reuse the potting compost in which you plant annuals, certainly once more, and I am sure a lot of gardeners do. Simply remove the old plants and add slow-release fertiliser to the compost—use quantities recommended on the packet—and carry on. In practice you have to be a little bit cautious, since the soil may have become contaminated with goodness-knows-what. Most dreadful might be the presence of eggs or grubs of the appalling vine weevil, which could make short work of the roots of the next tenants in the pots. If you suspect you have a vine-weevil problem, you could empty the compost on to plastic sheets and let it dry out (or allow it to be picked over by hungry robins) before spreading it around your garden beds and borders, or even add it to a compost bin or heap or to a pile of grass clippings—all grist to the horticultural mill, one way or another.

COMPOSTING FOR BEGINNERS

The late John Cushnie, a regular on *Gardeners' Question Time,* liked to be provocative. Plastic compost bins are, he said, hopeless. This was in response to a complaint from a woman that the kitchen waste regularly dumped in her bin looked just the same three or four months later as it did the day it went in. To me John's unequivocal statement was like a red rag to a bull. With a little careful management, plastic compost bins, with which so much of the population is taking its first hesitant, sometimes faltering composting steps, can produce good compost. If you have a plastic bin, have another one if you can, so that one has time to mature. Stand them where the sun gets at them (heat is important), on soil not paving, and use weed-smothering membrane or metal mesh (to stop intrusion by tree roots and rodents respectively).

The base
Compost bins and heaps should really only be built on a porous base, and ideally (but less essentially) there should be a drainage/aeration layer—twigs or small logs covered with metal mesh—between the compost and the soil below. Although worms and woodlice and other essential little beasts will manage to get into all sorts of surprising places—I once found a colony of worms hiding under a wooden seat 10ft (3m) up in a tree house—the general composting activity is far quicker and healthier if bins are on a soil base.

If you stir your compost regularly (see below), most of it will be ready at the same time. Forget accessing it through those silly little doors at the bottom: just lift the bin right off its contents, use the 95 per cent that is ready, put the bin back over the rest and start again—a messy Sunday morning job, once every few months. The bin contents always sink dramatically in the final stages. Robert emailed to say he is amazed that he gets so little compost out of his bin. Is something eating it? I suspect not. The fact is that compost just shrinks dramatically. A 'full' bin, once properly rotted, yields about a third of its original volume.

Wet and dry
Many bins 'fail' because they are either too dry or too wet and paper is the most readily available commodity that will help to regulate this. Compost aficionados bang on about the carbon/nitrogen balance. Basically, for every thick layer of anything

171

wet or green that goes into the bin you should add an equivalent amount of something dry and dead. This can be straw or shredded cardboard, but shredded paper is the most readily available and it is startling how much your bin will absorb. Paper shredders are not expensive, and can often be found on special offer. If the bin becomes too dry (a rarity in my experience), water it or—as so many garden media-types delight in telling you—pee in it.

Plastic bins will absorb an enormous amount of woodier prunings if they are shredded to reduce their bulk by about 80 per cent. For those with shrubs, trees or hedges, a garden shredder is a useful investment and can be shared between several households. Once regarded as unsociably clattery, the 'quiet' ones are quite different animals (I have an electric Bosch workhorse which has been happily chewing up my prunings without deafening anyone for the past seven years or so). Woody prunings take longer to rot down and the resulting compost is coarser (so no good for potting), but is great for mulching.

Insect life

It pays to remember that insect and animal life in the bin is all part and parcel of the rotting down process. Hoards of woodlice are just doing their thing, as are ants. Slugs and snails are too—although you can (if you are not organic with a capital 'O') water the heap with Scott's Liquid Slugclear to sort them out. Clouds of tiny flies indicate the heap is too wet (so do more stirring, have an extra go with the paper shredder and keep the lid off the bin for a day or two).

Stir it up

Finally, and most importantly—absolutely everyone with a plastic bin needs a compost aerator/stirrer with which to mix the contents on a regular basis—probably once a week, or whenever there is any major addition to the bin. It is really hard to do this essential job efficiently with an ordinary garden fork because the top openings of bins are so high and narrow. Stirring the bin at least halves the rotting time of the compost and irons out most of the potential problems at the same time. I have had enthusiastic feedback from readers who have tried these gadgets. Darlac make a super-efficient version with a double-sided handle and a larger pair of 'blades'.

COMPOSTING MILDEWED PLANTS

Here is a particularly relevant query from Myra in Leicester: as you cut things down in the autumn, can you put the remains of plants that have clearly been suffering from powdery mildew in your compost heap?

In theory it is not a good idea, but it really

depends on what kind of compost heap you have. A real hotty of a heap should cook out any nasty fungal things. And mildews are fairly specific and are unlikely to be 'spread' via compost mulches, etc. Also remember, a plant that has suffered this year from mildew will almost certainly suffer again next year anyway if conditions such as overcrowding and insufferable drought prevail—unless you manage to control the disease by spraying early with a systemic fungicide as a preventative measure. If this doesn't reassure you and you have the kind of heap that only rarely heats up because it does not receive large quantities of chopped greenery at any one time, then put your mildew-y green waste into your local council green recycling bags or wheelie bins: the temperatures achieved in their composting process are invariably consistently higher than anything we can achieve at home (see page 176).

GETTING RATTY

There are those—mostly probably non-gardeners—who hold us compost-makers largely responsible for the current rodent uprising from which it would seem from your letters and emails that we are suffering. I feel that this is probably somewhat unfair, but here for gardeners are some rat facts that I have gathered from personal experience (being an avid compost-maker and sometime poultry-keeper) of which we should be aware. I am sure there are other rat facts—yes, I do know they are vermin; that they brought us the bubonic plague and are responsible for the spread of Weil's disease.

1. Rat (and other rodent) numbers have increased massively, largely because of a series of mild winters.

2. Many gardeners are unaware of (or determinedly turn a blind eye to) the fact that rats will frequently take up residence in compost heaps and bins and old undisturbed grass piles simply because they provide ideal warm, sheltered places for them to hang out.

3. Rats are far more likely to do this, in fact almost certain to do so, near restaurants with badly maintained dustbin areas, and if there are chickens or even pet rabbits kept in the vicinity and especially if there are well-stocked bird tables in local gardens. They will nest and breed near any source of easy food.

4. Realistically there is not an awful lot we gardeners can do—we are all wise to the fact, that in order to minimise the likelihood of attracting rats, meat, fish, cheese and egg-based kitchen waste should never go into compost heaps or bins.

Personally I am simply not prepared to advise people to stop making compost, to stop feeding their garden birds or to get rid of their beloved rabbits or poultry. This would constitute giving in to what amounts (in my view) to near paranoia, based principally on the fact that we just don't like rats because of past associations.

If the rat population in an area gets to really upsetting levels, groups of concerned neighbours should stop blaming us gardeners and simply get together and call in a rat catcher every six months or so. As I see it, this really is the only (albeit fairly temporary) solution.

175

COUNCIL COMPOST TIPS

What happens, asks emailer Beryl, to the hotchpotch of appalling weeds and other garden grot that she and many others dump in the 'green bins' at the council tip? Is it properly rotted down, so that all the weed seeds and bits of ground-elder root are really killed? Or are the poor suckers who buy it back as 'compost' from their local councils likely to get more than they bargained for?

Similar thoughts have crossed my mind, so I thought I should do some digging around to find out. In layman's language, the process goes something like this. The green waste from council bins is composted in 1,000 ton lots that are kept at a constant temperature of 70°C (158°F) for approximately two weeks. There are no chemical accelerators added, and some of each hot batch is extracted to start further batches. During this time the compost is in fact so hot that weed seeds and any nasty roots are 'cooked' out, as are any pesticides, weedkillers and any other chemicals likely to be used by gardeners. The second stage involves keeping the compost at a constant temperature of between 55–60°C (131–140°F) for up to one and a half months. After a further four months it is sieved and graded, and tested to see if anything is still alive enough to grow or germinate in it. It is also subjected to pH tests and assessed as to its nutrient content. The resulting compost is used extensively in the salad production industry, and is also available to the public under the name of Pro-Grow. It has also been used in various high-profile national enterprises such as the Eden Project.

COMPOSTING WEEDS

Jim from Southport wants to know whether or not it is safe to put weeds with their roots attached into his compost bin, having heard conflicting stories from local gardeners.

The answer to this one is 'yes and no'. If the weeds in question are tricky, invasive-rooted perennials such as bindweed and ground elder, they really need to be thoroughly dried off and dead before they are added to the bin with other composing material, so that they are definitely incapable of regenerating. But be wary of doing this with all your weeds. For example, if you leave weeds such as willow herb and groundsel that are flowering lying around on the ground 'to dry', they are still capable of ripening and dispersing their wind-borne seeds even after they have been uprooted.

Unless you have a super-efficient bin that really heats up and stays hot for a long time, some seeds inevitably survive the composting process, which means that any weeds that have already made their seeds can be a bit of a composting liability. Hazell from Maidstone complains that she has a huge problem with seeds surviving in her uncovered timber-framed compost heaps. By covering the heaps she would trap in more heat—which will both speed up the composting considerably and kill a lot of the weed seeds into the bargain. I use thick black butyl rubber to cover compost bins—off-cuts of pond liner.

And finally, if you are trying to get rid of couch grass, it is safer to compost it completely separately. Couch grass roots are shallow, so you can effectively remove them completely by slicing away the top 2–3in (5–8cm) of soil with a spade or turfing iron, stacking it up and covering it with moisture- and light-excluding black plastic for a year or so. The resulting compost should be rich and couch-grass free.

GREY AREAS

Emailer Barbara has read that paper printed with coloured ink should not be composted (although ripped-up card and shredded paper get the thumbs up, as we all know). So what about multi-coloured newspaper, she asks? This is a rather grey area. Certainly some years back all printing ink was a bit suspect, but since then the printing industry has cleaned up its act. Now, unwilling to get bogged down in the science of it all, I simply tend to avoid putting shiny coloured magazine paper in with the compost, because it seems less absorbent, and takes longer to break down.

Florence writes to ask why the white biodegradable bags that she uses for her kitchen compost refuse to break down properly as she had expected them to, so that her otherwise perfect stuff is blighted by the stringy white remnants of them. That is because, I am reliably informed, biodegradable does not necessarily mean compostable—and, I was reminded, because of the difference in methods used, there is even a difference between 'compostable' and 'home compostable'.

My conclusion is that, not only are there 'grey areas' to composting, if you are not careful you can get bogged down in the science of it all and let the whole thing become just another giant stress-inducing can of worms. Avid composters should not let themselves be discouraged.

October

STAGGERING WORK IN THE BORDER

It is one—or should I say 'another'?—of those times in the year when the sheer amount of work that awaits outside can be seriously overwhelming. The once-lovely borders have not perked up completely since they sagged in the heat of July. Despite all my good intentions to cut things back, keep things going and plant, each year, more of the lovely daisies—blue asters and russet and yellow rudbeckias—that do so well, flower so late and keep on going for weeks, there is an awful lot of leaning beige out there. After a busy summer, the shed looks as though it has been turned over by burglars and the greenhouse, shortly to receive its winter population of half-hardy perennials, is still full of the crusty remains of a spring propagation fest that is just a distant memory. It is difficult to know where to start.

It is true that early October, when the soil is still warm, is a really good time for all that necessary division and sorting-out of perennials, and if you have a lot of new planting to do it is best to get on with it. But—dare I say it? Yes, I will—if you are, like me, pressed for time and short on enthusiasm, most of the herbaceous stuff in beds and borders can wait awhile. The big 'autumn' clear up can be done bit-by-bit, bed-by-bed, in mild weather throughout the winter. In my garden I hack down the things as they start to list sideways or look generally wrecked, or I just clear spaces where I

180

need to plant little crowds of alliums (around now) or tulips in late autumn. Anything still standing is felled before growth re-starts in earnest in February when, to the accompaniment of a pair of tuneless mistle thrushes, I set to work optimistically in the wan sunshine. Overzealous spreaders are controlled, casualties noted, biennial seedlings culled and re-shuffled to fill spaces and a general fertiliser and/or compost is spread around. The borders, finally cleaned up, turn the corner for yet another year.

AUTUMN SCENTS

I have really appreciated the scent of my **Nicotiana** *sylvestris on warm evenings. Although we can never take our Indian summers for granted, what other scented plants can I grow next year that will flower late in the season?*
Kay, by email

Evening-scented plants are principally pollinated by moths—which is why they are so often glow-in-the-dark white. The plants that spring to mind are *Acidanthera murielae* (strictly speaking, now renamed *Gladiolus murielae*)—a delicate, white-flowered, rather tender gladiolus—available to buy as bulbs now. Pot them up, keep them virtually dry in the greenhouse for the winter but don't expect much activity until next June. Another early autumn winner in my own garden is always *Cimicifuga racemosa*. This has also been renamed and is now called *Actaea*

181

simplex. It is a clumpy perennial that produces stunning tall, white flower spikes around now that smell deliciously sweet. There is an interestingly dark-leaved form. White perennial stocks will produce an autumn flush of scented flowers if deadheaded in June, and of course there are the Rugosa roses that, if deadheaded after their first flush of flowers, may still be producing the odd bloom alongside their gorgeous red hips. But the surprise performer at this time of year—I caught a whiff of its lily-of-the-valley scent as I passed by a front garden the other day—is the evergreen shrub *Elaeagnus × ebbingei*. This large toughie of a shrub, excellent for hedging, will go on producing its tiny, powerfully scented flowers on and off all autumn and on into winter.

THE MOLES ARE BACK

Lovable moles in literature have us all fooled—until we start gardening. It is hard, even now, not to admire these endearing little chaps with their wiggly, piggy-pink noses, whose coats are so wonderfully slinky despite all that muddy tunnelling.

By now I have probably heard just about all your deterrents and 'solutions'. Despite the insertion into mole runs of empty bottles, windmills (and other clattery wind-driven gizmos); oil-soaked rags, garlic and mothballs; pipes to discharge mower exhaust fumes or mighty zwooshes of water; the planting of smelly bulbs; or even 'controlled' explosions of doubtful legality that cause minor earth tremors, the moles don't seem to bat an eyelid. However determined we are, moles seem to be more so at ignoring or sidestepping deterrents.

Brutal though it may sound, the only way to get rid of moles is to trap them. Many reluctant readers try this last resort, and many fail because it is so hard to locate the permanent, deep travelling runs (as opposed to the shallow feeding runs that end in molehills) in which the traps must be set. These, I have learnt, are often to be found following the lines of hedges, and can be precisely located by putting a slim metal probe (an extra-long kebab stick in my case) into the ground at intervals. Disposable gloves must be worn when setting traps, to keep human scent off them, and the traps themselves placed in the runs very lightly so that they will spring shut (aagh!) cleanly. It is important to exclude all light by carefully replacing chunks of turf and putting an inverted bucket over the site. Even with expert tuition from an old hand, I have only managed to trap one mole. The 'humane' traps (which lock the moles in boxes so you can release them—where, exactly?) are probably even more difficult to place without the moles becoming wise to them.

An interesting snippet of information about mole spurge (*Euphorbia lathyris*) from Jennie Maillard from Usual and Unusual Plants of Hailsham in East Sussex. She is reliably informed by Timothy Walker from the Oxford Botanic Garden (so great a boffin is he that even his title— Horti Praefectus—is in Latin) that, in the past, the plant's sap was used on the sort of moles you find on your skin and through the years it became inexplicably but perhaps understandably connected with the elimination of tunnelling moles.

And finally... I cannot believe that Patrick is not just winding us all up. He urges anyone whose newly turfed and much-loved lawn is smothered in irritating worm casts that one easy solution to the problem might be to introduce... moles. Yes, the very idea made me smile, too.

WHITHER HERBS?

An awful lot of new little herb plants have a very short life. Lumped together by the suppliers as if they were a real horticultural family, too many minute plants are sold pre-potted together in unsuitable peat-based compost in inappropriately tiny 'strawberry pots' or some such. Typically we may be offered a 4in (10cm) tall cutting of bay (a tree, eventual height 20ft/6m), cheek by jowl with a similar-sized mini-frill of parsley (a shade-tolerant, 1ft/30cm high biennial needing deep, rich soil) and a little sprig of thyme (a shrublet that needs year-round full sun and sharp drainage). No wonder so many fizzle out after a couple of months.

Trying to do things on a slightly bigger scale—growing herbs 'formally' in their own patch in a small garden—is hard, too. As many have discovered, you really need to devote a lot of space to them in order to grow enough of the most useful culinary herbs. The best formal herb gardens are always quite large and grand, benefiting from full sun and relying heavily on swanky structure for their looks—a formal layout here, beds separated by lovely brick paths there, and yards of smart box edging just about everywhere. The herbs themselves (work-a-day ones frequently interspersed with architectural giants such as lovage and angelica) have plenty of space to run to seed and flop everywhere without overwhelming each other. While these are wonderful places to be, full of hot scent and buzzing with bees and hoverflies, much of their charm comes from their baked, colourless shabbiness—which could drive you wild if it was in your face all year round.

For those with less space and rather more practical culinary ambitions, I think herbs are best planted in among other plants with similar needs, rather than put together in a doll's-sized herb garden that doesn't work, and since they will thus be grown for ornament not just for cooking, it makes sense to grow varieties with coloured leaves: purple sage, golden marjoram, variegated apple mint (far less rampant than plain green), bronze fennel and so on.

Parsley and chives like deep moist soil and make good bedfellows in dappled shade. I find these kitchen staples both need to be grown in quantity since I use them so often. Parsley—a biennial that runs to seed in its second season—can be slow to germinate. I started off my now plentiful supply by buying a few ready-potted seedlings, planting them out carefully (they hate root disturbance) and letting one or two plants seed around. Little parsley plantlets appear in late summer and are given fleece protection over winter—so far the population has renewed itself reliably. I also keep a large deep pot of parsley in a shady spot right by the back door for when the weather is too lousy to nip down the garden.

Shrubby thymes, rosemaries and sages need as much sun as you can give them, and sharp drainage. They are at home growing in a hot spot among other aromatic plants such as cistuses, artemisias and lavender. Tarragon is messy to look at, but needs sun and lots of space to thrive. Tall and ornamental fennel is happy in a border (but watch out for invasive seedlings), as are various marjorams. Coriander runs to seed at the drop of a hat, and needs to be sown every few weeks and cut frequently, and basil has too short a season in our cold climate, unless you are a dedicated greenhouse gardener. No wonder so many of us buy it in pots from the supermarkets.

PERENNIAL STOCK—CHAPTER AND VERSE

I briefly waxed lyrical about it once, and Veronica from Loughborough subsequently tracked down a young 8in (20cm) tall plant of a white shrubby perennial stock (*Matthiola incana alba*). She is disappointed that although it has grown and looks quite healthy it has not flowered, and recently its lower leaves are going yellow. Has she done something wrong? Is her plant, in its 'optimistically large' pot, trying to tell her it needs to go indoors for the winter? She needs to know more about this hard-to-find plant and feels other readers may too.

I presume Veronica's new 'baby' is a young seedling, and young plants of perennial stock don't flower in their first year and sometimes not even in their second. But they do start to make an almost shrubby framework topped with attractive, rather exotic-looking rosettes of grey foliage. As they mature, and in any periods of drought in the summer, the plants' lower leaves invariably go yellow and eventually drop (or can be tweaked off by the more fastidious among us) as the plant's stem grows taller. Plants will last for maybe three years, by which time they will be around 3ft (1m) tall and will have produced numerous flowering side shoots. Their innate gauntness can be hidden behind other plants.

Eventually plants just run out of steam, but before they do, each year stunningly scented flowering starts around May and can be prolonged by high-potash feeding and prompt removal of older leaves and seed heads. However, if allowed to drop seed, little plants may show up in odd corners and these can be lifted carefully and potted up, eventually to replace ageing 'parents'. For what it is worth, I have had greater success with this 'laissez-faire' method of propagation than I have by doing things 'by the book'—taking cuttings in late summer or sowing seed in trays. Strong, soil-based compost, John Innes No 3, suits mature permanently container-grown plants, but I put the odd plant here or there—by paths and near doorways—in my ordinary, quite heavy, more or less neutral garden soil. Perennial stocks are hardy and can be left outside all winter—although frosted foliage looks temporarily limp and dreadful, rather like that of shrubby euphorbias. Being of the brassica (cabbage) family, plants are attractive to the large (cabbage) white butterfly, with potentially disastrous results.

WOOD-BE MULCH

We have recently thinned out and cleared up an area of our garden that had become an untidy piece of untended woodland, removing an overgrown holly tree. We are now in the process of planting it up with shrubs with the intention of making it into a woodland garden. We had the holly tree trunk and branches chipped. Is there any reason why we can't now use the chippings (which are mixed with holly leaves) to mulch the shrubs?
Graham, by email

In their virgin, uncomposted state the chippings will be ideal for making woodland paths, or perhaps for mulching areas you do not intend to plant up with woodland ground cover—hellebores, ferns, etc. But I would suggest that you let the pile of chippings sit around for at least six months, preferably a year, before you use them as mulch around newly planted shrubs since, as wood chippings compost, they deplete the soil beneath them of nitrogen. You will notice that the pile of chippings has probably already started to heat up. The hotter it gets the better, and when it cools down it will be invaded by moulds and bacteria that will partially compost it for you. Once it has got this far, it will be useful soil conditioner and mulch, but in the meantime, I would suggest that you use pre-composted bark, leaf mould or home-made compost—something that is already rotted—around your shrubs.

An additional word here about composted bark—the praises of which are not sung enough, I feel. All garden soils are improved, as we know, by being bulked out with organic matter, and none of us seems to be able to generate enough of the right kind of stuff. I now use composted bark extensively as a mulch and also dig it in along with quantities of grit to improve both drainage and moisture retention. The bark is not particularly 'foody' (I can always add nutrients in other ways), but it has a lovely texture and, I gather, a neutral pH (unlike mushroom compost). Surprisingly, I don't see bags of it around in garden centres much, so I buy it in bulk.

SLUG-PROOF PLANTS

I asked for readers' help in compiling a list of plants that they had found were resistant—perhaps that is a bit strong, 'less attractive' is a better choice of words—to slugs. While we all hate snails too, it is slugs that do most of the heartbreaking damage to emerging plants. It is not intended to be comprehensive or 'official' in any way and comes with no guarantees and is no doubt very incomplete—but still useful.

There was some dissent in the ranks, however. Plantsman Richard Zatloukal disagreed with my assertion that snails don't chomp bergenias, that they merely lurk in gangs under the leathery canopy during dry weather. His mother's bergenias in Provence were nibbled to bits, he said. I think I know the reason and I have a few words of my immaculate Franglais for Richard's mother: vigne weevil—cherchez et clobberez les grubs dans le soil elsewhere, et Robert est votre oncle.

Achillea
Aconitum
Ajuga
Alchemilla
Allium moly
Alyssum
Anaphalis
Aquilegia
Arabis
Astilbe
Astrantia
Ballota
Begonia
Bergenia
Calendula
Campanula
Caryopteris
Catmint
Corydalis
Crocosmia
Crocus
Cyclamen
Dianthus
Diascia
Dierama
Dicentra
Erigeron
Erysimum
Eschscholzia
Euphorbia characias
Euphorbia griffithii
Evening primrose

Ferns
Filipendula
Forget-me-not
Foxgloves
Fuchsia
Gaura
Geranium palmatum and some other cranesbills
Golden rod
Gypsophila
Heathers
Helianthemum
Hellebores
Heuchera
House leeks
Inula hookeri
Japanese anemones
Lamium
Lavender
Leucanthemum
Leycesteria formosa
Lobelia
Lychnis coronaria
Lysimachia
Marjoram
Mint
Musk mallow
Nigella
Osteospermum
Paeonia
Pansies
Pelargonium

190

Penstemon
Phlox paniculata
Phuopsis
Phygelius
Pinks
Platycodon
Primulas
Pulmonaria
Rudbeckia
Roses
Saxifraga × urbium
Schizostylis

Scilla
Sedums
Sidalcea
Sisyrinchium
Stachys lanata
Tellima
Thalictrum
Thyme
Valerian
Verbascum
Verbena bonariensis

SHRUBS FOR BOGGY SOIL

Part of my garden stays very wet in the winter and although it cannot be classed as a real 'bog', it has very heavy soil. I have tried to improve the soil with not much success, and while some of the plants I have put in are doing reasonably well, I have lost some conifers (which turned brown at the bottom before dying). Are there some shrubs that would actually like these conditions?
Lynn, by email

Choosing plants for winter-sodden ground like this is quite a problem, since the underlying clay that often causes it makes life tough for plant roots, and does not retain moisture well in the summer months. Your soil improvement (presumably with 50/50 organic matter and grit) will perhaps have increased the summer moisture-retention quality, without really fundamentally improving drainage. For this you would have to put in land drains, which—unless the area is sizeable—is a step too far for most gardeners, I suspect.

Have you had a look at the vast family of willows? Willows come in all shapes and sizes, including some dwarf shrubby ones. Even some of the larger ones can be kept smallish by stooling (cutting right down to a stump) every other February. There are some varieties with most attractive colouring to their leaves and stems—look out for *Salix elaeagnos*, with the finest, silvery leaves, and dark-stemmed *S. purpurea* 'Nancy Saunders'. Then of course there are the cornuses, who seem to revel in having wet feet. Again there are several eye-catching varieties (*Cornus alba* 'Elegantissima' has clean-looking, variegated foliage) and they all have good autumn colour as well as bright stems in winter. *Viburnum opulus*, another shrub with great autumn foliage colours which has, in addition, scarlet, jewel-like berries, is another moisture-lover, although it is a bit of a whopper. There is a smaller variety, *V. opulus* 'Compactum', that would be more suitable if space is limited.

POTS OF LILIES

I have a few pots planted up with scented lilies—a great joy in my courtyard garden. What is the best way of looking after them? Should they be re-potted each year? What

should I do with them in the winter? Do they need feeding—and with what?
Caroline, Lewes, East Sussex

Growing lilies in pots is probably the easiest, most rewarding way to grow them, but it is not all plain sailing, as many a disappointed gardener knows. Pests can be a real problem. Right now you should be worrying about the evil (vine) weevil, or rather its fat, white, c-shaped grubs, which can infest the soil in all garden pots and, unseen during the coming weeks and months, completely destroy plant roots and lily bulbs (see also April, page 43). If you have evergreens with lower leaves notched and nibbled (the work of the adult weevils) I would now drench the soil in all your pots, where they will have laid their eggs, with Provado Vine Weevil Killer as a precaution. This awful pest can play havoc in small, sheltered courtyard gardens such as yours. Provado, which contains systemic imidacloprid, is also useful in the war against the scarlet lily beetle, which will be going underground at around this time for winter hibernation.

So much for the horror story, now for the rest. Lily bulbs don't necessarily need re-potting every year if they are in roomy, heavy, clay pots containing gutsy, soily compost such as John Innes No 3, with a little added leaf mould or compost. You can gently scrape away the top few of inches of soil next spring and replace it with fresh stuff, and re-pot them the year after perhaps. When you do re-

193

pot them, it may be a good idea to set them at
a slight angle in the soil, with a little grit
underneath them, which, I am assured, helps
to prevent them from rotting, and make sure
they are covered by at least 4in (10cm) of soil.
A liquid feed once a fortnight while they are
in growth is all they need, and what is more,
lilies are hardy, and will not need to be
overwintered indoors. But bring the pots
close to the house and make sure they do not
spend the winter waterlogged, sitting in
puddles.

Once they have flowered you should cut
off the swelling seedpods, and as the leaves
and stems become tatty cut them down by
half—the remaining few inches eventually
just disintegrate and can then be gently
pulled away from the bulb below. When you
remove any supporting canes (which are
generally necessary to cope with the weight of
flowers in the height of summer), replace
them with short markers so that you do not
accidentally stab the bulbs when you insert
new canes next spring.

TRICKY ACHILLEAS

Hilary from Chelmsford finds it hard to grow achilleas, of which she is particularly fond. They only really work for her in their first year and never 'fatten up'. Is there a knack to it, she asks? I think the answer is to replant them every other year, giving them plenty of rich compost and a fistful of a general fertiliser as you do so. I tend to agree with her that those lovely new varieties in subtle shades are rather feeble. The best varieties, I find, are the old ones: *Achillea* 'Moonshine' is a goodie—and a lovely one I got from Great Dixter, 'Lucky Break', seems to have a lot of guts, too.

BEGINNER'S LUCK

I am definitely not a gardener, but I was persuaded to buy little plants of morning glory at a boot fair (with no instructions, of course), and planted them in a large pot on my balcony. After a slow start they climbed up an old trellis and flowered beautifully throughout August, with new blooms (like blue bindweed) greeting me each morning. I feel this was certainly 'beginner's luck'. Will they flower again next year?
Jeanette, Poole, Dorset

The lovely pale blue morning glory (*Ipomoea*) is, unlike bindweed, a tender, quite fussy, annual plant and yours will have most probably died by now. However, maybe we can make a gardener of you. Saving seed and growing annuals is where many of us start.

On the dead stems of your plants you will notice that the old flowers will have left behind swollen seedpods, each containing a few black seeds not unlike apple pips. Collect some of the 'pips' and store them somewhere cool but dry (in an old envelope, perhaps, but make sure you write on the outside to remind you of the contents). In early May next year, soak some of the seeds in a saucer of water for 24 hours, and then carefully press them (three seeds to a pot, to be on the safe side) into the surface of some small pots of previously moistened multi-purpose compost. Cover the seeds lightly with sand and then put cling film over the pots until you see leaves appearing. Remove the film, and keep the pots on a bright windowsill, but not in direct sun, making absolutely sure that the compost does not dry out. You could remove the weaker seedlings from each pot at this point. When the remaining plants have made their second set of leaves they will want to start to climb, and you could transplant them with great care into a larger pot (as you did this year). Night temperatures will not be reliable enough for them until at least the first week of June, so don't be in too much of a hurry to put them outside permanently. Of course, if all this sounds a bit too much like real gardening, you could always take pot luck at a boot fair again...

TREE TIES

Why do some people tie their trees with stakes at an angle, some use short straight stakes, and others long? Is there a right and wrong way to tie trees, and how long should the stakes be left in place?
Mark, Bury St Edmunds

It is customary to use slanting tree stakes on container-grown trees, and straight stakes on bare-rooted ones. The reasons are utterly logical: it would be extremely easy to damage the roots of a container-grown tree by banging a stake right through the middle of the root ball. However, a stake driven in at an angle after the tree is planted will prevent this happening. The top of the stake should face into the wind, so that when the tree is buckled to it (using a purpose-made plastic tie, with the plastic 'nut' between the stake and the tree) there is no danger of the trunk being injured by the two chafing against each other. Straight stakes can be used on bare-rooted trees, and should be knocked in place once the tree is in the correct position in its planting hole, and before it is earthed up. To be sure that it will do the job properly, 2ft (60cm) should be below ground and about the same above. The stake should again be placed on the windward side of the tree.

These days short stakes are used more often than long ones. Research has shown that young tree trunks will thicken up more quickly where they are allowed to bend a little in the wind from early on in their development, so unless the tree is quite tall when you plant it and planted in a particularly vulnerable site, it may not be strictly necessary to use a stake at all. Where they are used, stakes and ties should be checked and adjusted at the beginning and end of each growing season. Certainly after three years the tree should have made enough new roots to become stable, and stakes should then be removed completely. Trees that have been planted then abandoned and finally burst from their ties or, worse, become strangled by them are a sorry sight in any garden.

CLEMATIS ALL YEAR ROUND?

You can't *really* have clematis flowering in your garden all the year round, can you, asked Ruth from Kent? The answer is 'not quite, but nearly'.

Much depends on regional climatic subtleties, of course, but the year can kick off with *Clematis cirrhosa* var. *balearica*, a ferny-leaved evergreen scrambler that can flower in January. Hard on its heels will be the scented, rampant *C. armandii*—another evergreen, but with an infuriating habit of hanging on to its old leaves which just hang there, brown and leathery. For this reason *armandii* needs skilful management—late spring pruning or the careful 'weaving' of the new growth over the old. Other early birds (March/April) and far easier to accommodate are the compact clematis *C.* × *cartmanii* 'Joe' and close relations such as 'Pixie' (also evergreen) which will readily grow in tubs and scramble over a 3–4ft (1–1.2m) high support.

By April or May the flowers of *C. macropetala* and *C. alpina* will be nodding delicately at us from their happy vantage point up trees, and we are also getting into *Clematis montana* territory. There are many *montanas* to choose from: the classic 'Elizabeth' has pale pink flowers, var. *rubens* 'Tetrarose' has darker flowers and foliage, while my favourite var. *wilsonii* is white-flowered with a strong, heady scent. This one flowers later than the others, well into June—by which time, of course, all those ultra-showy cultivars will have been doing their stuff for a month or so. 'Nelly Moser' is one of the earliest and is followed by numerous rather loud things with flowers the size of coffee-saucers: 'Lasurstern', 'Lord Nevill' and the double-flowered 'Vyvyan Pennell' are just a few of those on offer. Growing well and given a tidy-up after flowering, they may produce a few more flowers in early autumn.

The best of the bunch are still to come. In late June or early July *C.* 'Jackmanii' and the smaller-flowered wilt-resistant viticella hybrids burst on the scene. Viticellas are regarded as easy to grow because they can be simply pruned down to knee height each spring. Once established, such gems as 'Madame Julia Correvon' (rich red), 'Purpurea Plena Elegans' (with flowers like small blobs of muted purple crumpled tissue paper) and 'Alba Luxurians' (crisply greenish white) will provide masses of colour for several weeks.

Late summer sunlight flatters the yellow-flowered members of the tribe that bloom in September, the best known of which is 'Bill MacKenzie'. And last of all are the autumn-flowering tree scramblers, such as the tiny-flowered, frothy *C. flammula*, which can fill a garden with scent until late October. Then, I am afraid, it is all over. Except that all these latecomers have silvery fluffy seed heads that linger through the winter—almost as good value as the flowers, after all.

ACCELERATING THE AGEING PROCESS

Pam feels she is swimming against the tide. While she reads a lot of advice given to gardeners about getting rid of all sorts of moss, algae and lichen, she wants to grow some, quickly, over the locally quarried, weathered grey stones in her new little waterfall. Is there a knack, a short cut, she asks? She is so impatient; she has even toyed with the idea of transplanting moss from her hanging baskets, but does not know how it would cling....

I find it quite amusing that some gardeners relish newly completed garden works—sparkling ponds, pristine fences (re-oranged every year) over which neighbours' plants are not allowed to trespass, power-washed patios off which you could eat your dinner every day of the year—while others (and I am afraid I am one) will go to any lengths to make a garden look as old as time. So although there are no real short cuts, I will go into some detail as to how you can add some essence of neglected dingly dell to your garden.

Moss and its close relations algae and lichen are all spread via air or water. The more porous the surface, and the more constantly damp (and shaded) the site, the quicker the growth will be, so I suspect that Pam's weathered rocks will inevitably go green within a few months because of their constant exposure to the splashes from the waterfall. An unwanted side effect will probably be some form of algal growth in the water, unfortunately.

Glaringly new pots and small statues will go green after a dunk (for a few weeks) in a murky pond. Or they can be painted with a soil and cow manure slurry or yoghurt. (Someone told me that Prince Charles had thus daubed the amended front of Highgrove in order to assist the ageing process. If so, it worked rather well.) A touch of peat or soil added to mortar on new brick walls takes the bright edge off things nicely. However, it should be remembered that all those very clever stone-look-alike bird baths and other garden ornaments do not 'age' easily with algae because, being resin, they are not porous.

RESCUE REMEDY FOR GHASTLY GRASS

My husband is really excited about having a lawn for the first time, but the small area of grass in our new garden is in a shocking state. He has sheared it and mowed it with a borrowed hover mower. It looks even worse and he now wants to dig it up and re-turf it. This seems rather drastic. Is there an alternative?
Sally, Colchester, Essex

Yes, but it involves a combination of hard graft and patience for a few months. Go out and buy your husband a lawn rake, a rotary mower with a grass collection box, an appropriate quantity of autumn lawn food

201

and a book on basic lawn care (*The Lawn Expert* from the Expert series by Dr D G Hessayon is as good as it gets).

The best thing your husband can do now is rake over the whole area to get out all the dead grass that may have formed a thick thatch underneath the mutilated greenery on this poor lawn. He will complain that it looks even worse—he will be absolutely right—but don't let him give up. He should then mow the grass on a fairly high setting and apply the autumn lawn fertiliser to strengthen the roots of the grass during the winter. It will still look pretty ropey (the autumn lawn food does nothing to stimulate growth), but because it seems that our grass grows for around eleven months of the year now, he should just keep at it and mow whenever the grass looks as though it needs it during mild, dry weather, always keeping the blades on a high setting.

The grass will start growing properly in March or April, at which time he can seed any serious bald patches and/or apply a high-nitrogen fertiliser to speed things up, and gradually lower the blade height. Weed growth will accelerate as well, of course, but regular mowing will see off a surprising number of these. The persistent ones that lie down when they see the mower coming—dandelion, creeping buttercup and plantain—can be spot weedkilled. If by this time your husband has turned into an obsessive lawn-fiend (as is highly likely), he can go the whole hog and treat the lawn with a selective lawn weedkiller or a weed-and-feed treatment. Oh yes, there is a whole world of fun to be had out there.

CERINTHE SEEDLINGS

Am I imagining things? My self-sown cerinthe seedlings that survived in the ground last winter grew into plants that didn't have the lovely colouring of their 'parents'. Was it the cold winter that did it? Should I save seed from them and start them off on a windowsill indoors this year?
Anthea, by email

I don't think you are imagining it; *Cerinthe major* 'Purpurascens' is definitely not the plant it was a decade or two ago.

This exotic-looking annual became an instant must-have when it first appeared, with its arching stems of glaucous foliage tipped with startling dusky mauve/sea-green bracts, in which nestled deep plum-purple bell-like flowers. At first precious seed was passed from one posh gardener 'in the know' to another. Then, bingo—mass production. Cerinthe is now available everywhere, generally sold as potted singletons in late spring. Many gardeners keep some of the masses of black seeds each plant produces and grow their own, and it will also seed itself about.

You were unlucky, however, and in a rather 'hit and miss' situation, definitely scored a 'miss' if none of your self-sown plants had that distinctive colouring. Having investigated the situation for myself, I can assure you that it has nothing whatsoever to do with the winter cold.

Plants such as this are grown originally from specimens that are, effectively, wonderful freaks of nature. Plain and simple *Cerinthe major* is actually a fairly unimpressive weedy plant from the Mediterranean, with vaguely spotty, only slightly glaucous leaves and bracts, with small pale-ish maroon bells that are edged yellow. It seems that if you keep your own seed, the plants you grow will gradually revert, with maybe just one or two seedlings bearing something akin to the distinctive colours of those stunning original plants. My advice is to start with fresh seed—most of the seed companies now stock it each year—and be prepared for a somewhat 'mixed bag'.

So alas this one is real, Anthea. Unlike the policemen who are 'getting younger' and the Marmite that doesn't taste the way it used to…

LOPPERS OR SECATEURS?

William's neighbour insists that their laurel hedge should be (tediously) pruned with secateurs and loppers. Will he seriously harm the hedge if he goes at his side with a hedge trimmer?

No, but there are two points to bear in mind. The cut edges of sheared or hedge-trimmed laurel leaves turn brown, which can look hideous for weeks if the hedge is not growing fast when cut. Painstaking pruning results in an instantly better-looking hedge—and gives the opportunity to remove older and dead wood from within it. The same applies to bay and other large-leaved evergreens.

November

BIG GREEN MONSTERS

Almost all of us inherit one or two outsize relics from previous gardeners at some stage—most probably out-of-control must-haves from an era of totally different plant 'fashions'. We enthusiastically grub out some of the worst huge horrors without hesitation—like the clutch of closely planted small Christmas trees and two ugly, shattered pampas grasses that I spent day after day attacking with a spade one hot summer. Friends that I visited are struggling with the remains of a large population of assorted coloured conifers planted in the 1970s as little ornamental things by previous owners of their large country garden. Some of those that escaped their first energetic cull are now taller than the house, threatening the very existence of some lovely wafty birches planted nearby and blocking the view of much of the garden and a local landscape studded with handsome native oak and beech. The trouble is, once these alien interlopers become larger than life, they tend to be perceived as so vital to the structure of the garden that owners simply find it impossible to see life beyond them—in more ways than one.

Somewhat embarrassingly, I often find myself trying to persuade various friends and acquaintances to take control of these massive aliens, be they ghastly overgrown conifers or (frequently) battered, ragged phormiums as wide

206

as they are tall. Originally planted as part of an altogether smaller garden tableau, decades later they nudge out most of their finer neighbours or start to black out the horizon. I find myself unable to keep my mouth shut, and urge these poor friends to get busy, remove (or radically prune) super-size eyesores, opening up the garden again and taking the opportunity to plant something new, to put their own stamp on things. I also find myself increasingly looking slightly sideways at more 'modern' gardens planted a decade or so ago with indiscriminately self-seeding grasses, rapidly expanding stripy, spiky things already revealing their ugly undercarriages, as well as bamboos that will soon run amok—if they haven't done so already. In fact the more I think of it, I realise how amazing it is that I am ever invited back to some of my friends' houses.

Planting a garden is one thing, maintaining the balance of power within it as it matures can be something altogether trickier. At least once a year we should all take a long, hard look at our gardens from every angle and, instead of just seeing the good bits, we should take off the blinkers and have a go at seeing what it is we might have lost sight of—before any big green monsters make us completely lose the ability to do so. And those of you who are totally resistant to change of any kind in the garden and who think this is a load of bossy, reactionary tosh should perhaps regard yourselves as extremely fortunate that you are not friends of mine.

MAGIC MUSHROOMS?

John from Glasgow wants to replace some of his old floribunda roses with new ones. He understands that there are always problems associated with this, and asks for advice.

Historically, as John is aware, new roses planted in old rose beds consistently fail to thrive. Extraordinarily perhaps, little is really understood by scientists about the causes of 'rose sickness' or 'replant disease' as it is now more often called. Prime suspects are some sort of dastardly microscopic soil-dwelling nematodes (to which established roses are presumed to become immune). There are also vague accusations about gardeners' desultory pre-planting preparation of the already exhausted soil in long-established rose beds. I have to say that, given the level of almost fanatical manuring, feeding and general soil-twiddling that dedicated rose people tend to go in for, I am inclined to be less than convinced by this idea.

But whatever the cause, until relatively recently the best advice on offer to overcome the frustrating problem of rose sickness was to replace completely the soil in the area designated for any new inmate of an old rose bed. And it had to be a lot of soil too—at least 2 cu ft (0.06 cu m) for each rose (although luckily it could simply be swapped with soil from another part of the garden). Or you could plant a new rose in good soil-based compost (or indeed suitably 'improved' garden soil from elsewhere), within a cardboard box of similar dimensions—the presumption being that by the

208

time the box had disintegrated the new rose would be big and tough enough to cope with whatever bogeybugs the unknown underworld beyond had in store for it.

At last it seems there is a solution available to us in the form of commercially produced mycorrhizal fungi—naturally occurring fungi that live unseen underground 'in the wild', benefiting plant growth, and now conveniently available in granular form out of a packet.

The science goes something like this: once the fungi make direct contact with the roots of most plants (there are exceptions, including brassicas), they attach themselves to them and grow outwards, searching for water and nutrients. The result is a symbiotic relationship between plant and fungi, leading to stronger, quicker and more disease-resistant plant growth. And it is now thought that introducing mycorrhizal fungi to the soil around the roots of new roses in old rose beds overcomes rose sickness problems. Roses, other shrubs and trees that are traditionally sold dormant and bare-rooted can have their nether regions dipped in a slurry of the stuff (a packet of wallpaper glue-style powder is included in the pack), while container-grown plants benefit from having their fine, hair-like roots very slightly exposed, so that they make direct contact with a mere sprinkle of the magic granules in the bottom of their planting holes. I applied mycorrhizal fungi to the bare roots of my roses and raspberries last year with pleasing results.

So John should hot foot it down to his local garden centre and seek out a packet of Rootgrow, as it is called. The product has now been enthusiastically endorsed by the RHS after extensive trials.

LEAVING LEAVES

Mr J L from Cheltenham 'did as he was told' last autumn and built a large (1 cu yd/1 cu m) leaf cage from chicken wire and wooden posts, lining the base with landscape fabric and filling it to the top with the oak, maple and birch leaves that littered his lawn and flowerbeds. While the leaves on the outer edges of the cage are still completely dry and unrotted, further into the heap the leaves, while still recognisable, are dark, damp and presumably half way to becoming leaf mould. The entire contents of the cage has, however, shrunk to around a quarter of its original volume. Should he pile this year's leaves on top of last year's leaves and let them break down together or… what?

To those who do not understand the satisfaction of making quantities of gloriously free leaf mould out of fallen leaves—manna from heaven for gardeners—this may seem like awful nitpicking, but I understand the dilemma completely. The answer is, of course, for Mr J L to 'do as he is told' again and go out and build another leaf heap as big as the last one—to accommodate this year's leaves. Of course, the last year's leaves that are already 'damp and half-rotted' can be used now as a useful, bulky, soil improver around the garden, but they will be even better if they are simply left to break down for another few months. In all likelihood they will have become truly gorgeous and crumbly by the time he really needs to mulch his shrubs or make great weed-free potting compost and so on in the coming spring.

The trouble with just piling newly fallen leaves on top of the old ones is that they don't all rot together evenly and you obviously then have great difficulty accessing the really good, older stuff at the bottom of the heap. It has taken me a long time to get into a sensible routine with my own autumn leaves—with which I am almost swamped for weeks on end in my shady little patch. One, or even two, cages were never going to be enough, so I now have three leaf cages sited invisibly behind evergreens in different parts of my garden. I cram two of them with freshly fallen leaves each autumn. Ten months later I spend an energetic half hour combining the amazingly shrunken contents of both to do their final bit of breaking down together in one cage. The result is a cage containing perfect leaf mould 'on tap' which I can raid, from time to time—and eventually empty—during the following spring and summer, while freeing up two whole cages again for a new lot of leaves. And so it will go on from year to year.

To reduce instantly the volume of larger autumn leaves and to considerably accelerate their rotting it really does help to use a leaf collector/shredder or to gather them up by mowing/chopping with a rotary mower.

Some leaves rot more easily than others—among the best are oak, beech and hornbeam. The leaves of tough evergreens take ages, and should only be added in small quantities to a leaf heap when thoroughly chopped. Similarly, the needles dropped by conifers are not particularly useful, and make an acid leaf mould. There are products

211

you can add to a heap to speed up the process, such as Biotal Compost Maker.

USEFUL TREES

Recommending trees to hide eyesores is not a task I relish much—in fact it is one that I try to avoid. Over the years, however, in order to encourage people not to plant a row of conifers to screen off the rest of the world, and in so doing sap the surrounding soil of all life and risk getting up the noses of neighbours, I have come up with a small list of useful trees which will distract the eye with their beauty and therefore soften the ugliest of views, while providing a certain level of privacy in the summer months. Planted with or without an underskirt of flowering evergreen and deciduous shrubs that can be pruned to strategic and manageable heights, a small tree with a light canopy will offend few and will generally enhance not just one's own garden, but all those in close proximity. In fact I would go so far as to say that every garden should contain at least one of the following—none of which is particularly rare or special, but all of which have at least two things going for them and have served me, and many other gardeners, well.

The front-runner for me is silver birch, the more silver the better: I love *Betula utilis* var. *jacquemontii* in particular. After only a few years this tree, with its bleached-white bark, forms a fantastic winter ghost—it is by far the most eye-catching thing in my garden between October and March. Next on the list is a winter-flowering prunus, *Prunus* × *subhirtella* 'Autumnalis', whose

212

pink or white flowers cheer up the dull grey months from time to time, and whose lightweight canopy turns a good coppery red in autumn. And then of course there are the amelanchiers, with their heavenly, dense but refined spring blossom and dark red berries (bullfinches permitting), followed by the reddest of red autumn leaves. For windy gardens, the rowans, with their autumn berries, are a good choice. Then there are trees with a larger foliage presence, also with good autumn colour, such as the fast-growing tulip tree, *Liriodendron tulipifera* (although you have to wait for 20 years or so for the 'tulips'), or sweet gum (*Liquidambar styraciflua*), and the slower-growing, criminally expensive but nicely named *Cercis canadensis* 'Forest Pansy', with plum-coloured leaves that go fabulously multi-coloured-orange in autumn. Last but by no means least on this tiny list is the walnut (*Juglans* spp.), since it has such wonderful, healthy-looking deep green foliage and a beautifully shaped canopy.

If there is one area of gardening where impulse buying definitely has no place, it is here. Whether you are adding to an existing tree population, choosing a singleton for a tiny garden or, like me, replacing ugly, damaged or inappropriate ones, it pays to do a lot of research and think hard before you buy. There is a good little book to help, with plenty of photographs, in which trees are categorised by size and seasons of interest: the RHS's *Garden Trees* (part of their Plant Guides series from Dorling Kindersley) should be on every gardener's bookshelf. It is now out of print but you might find it at the library or in a secondhand bookshop.

August, I find, is a good time to take one's eyes off the rest of the garden and look up at trees. I decided to take out more of my scraggy old leaning larches this year, and paced around tree nurseries sizing up more interesting replacements while they were in full leaf. Now is the time to buy and plant; I've had my assignation with the tree surgeons and started preparing the sites for my newcomers.

IN PRAISE OF URBAN GARDENERS

I have a great admiration for those who have gardening energy flowing through their veins but, for various reasons, have to contend not just with tiny spaces, cat-infested, exhausted urban soil, with domineering boundary fences and trees over which they have no control (providing copious shade yet, ironically, scarcely any privacy), but also face a non-stop proliferation of disruptive adjacent building works and invasive fumes from countless apparently obligatory barbecues.

In a former life I used to teach basic gardening. My protégées were almost all first-generation urban women faced with the task of embellishing small patches of greenery barely larger than a slice of toast (regarded of course as sacred turf by obsessive husbands who resented every inch their wives surreptitiously pinched in order to create the flower borders they craved). Most of them also had to deal with their children's erratic football skills and an inevitable hideous menagerie of garish plastic dross. In the background often lurked the terrifying influence of a grand provincial matriarch or two (whose distinctly 'hands-off' gardening style involved employing

214

faithful retainers to grow phalanxes of paeonies for the house, and to whom all yellow and orange flowers were anathema).

Despite all this, 'my women', as I refer to them with great affection to this day, showed a Tiggerish enthusiasm for the whole gardening thing. And once they had got through the compulsive-shopping phase (all plant nursery receipts were rigorously hidden from the aforementioned turfmaesters), stopped trying to cram the perceived obligatory threes and fives of everything into their little flower borders and generally playing chess with their plants on an almost daily basis, they settled down and took on board those important basics—about different kinds of light and shade (and what therefore would and what would not work) and about the extraordinary benefits of regularly improving their awful soil with well-rotted muck.

Above all I drummed into them the fundamental principles of shrub, rose and clematis pruning. Without these, I told them, gardening in such a confined space would have been unbearably disappointing. I am happy to say that many of my women have gone on to become excellent, sensitive gardeners—most of them, admittedly, now less spatially challenged. But the best gardens are not necessarily the biggest, I told them; they are the ones where the plants 'fit' and look comfortably, healthily in the right place.

And while there is bound to be an element of trial and error for beginners, satisfying urban gardening is learnt not so much by spending a lot of money or following anyone's rigid rules, but through the intelligent observation of other

215

gardeners' achievements. In the limited time we spent together we packed in some grander-scale inspiration, visiting Wisley, Sissinghurst, Great Dixter, and the garden and nursery of Beth Chatto. But I urged them then—and urge all urban gardeners now—to look also at small gardens that are close to home, owned by those who have mastered the same limitations as they face themselves. Many local charities run 'open garden' schemes, and of course the National Gardens Scheme's Yellow Book lists loads of urban gardens within their pages—more than two hundred of them in London alone.

BOX BLIGHT OR FOX BLIGHT?

Heidi sent me some pictures of two potted box balls, bought in May and since then kept on each side of her north-facing door. Both plants have developed large brown patches of foliage. She says that there is some evidence of (rather slow) new growth amid the brown leaves, and wonders if the damage was caused because the plants were not watered often enough before they were put in their permanent pots.

I think it might be helpful to look at all the possibilities on this one.

1. If the browning was down to a period of inconsistent watering, as Heidi suspects, the whole of the plants would have been affected. They would now look distinctly threadbare, with very obvious leaf-fall of the older leaves and only good, new growth on the shoot tips.

2. Box that is truly yellowing, rather than brown (it actually almost takes on an orange hue), is generally starving. Box is greedy and potted plants do best if fed annually with a general fertiliser (slow-release pellets are fine). From the pictures it is clear that the plants' remaining undamaged foliage is a good deep green, and since they have only recently been potted on, starvation is unlikely.

3. Could lack of light be to blame? Over time the back of each of these plants (nearest the north-facing wall) might well grow less vigorously than the side with more light, a problem easily prevented by turning the plants every so often, but this damage looks too extreme, and has happened too quickly, for this to be the cause.

4. There is a fairly strong chance, I feel—in view of the patchy nature of the damage and the fact that Heidi says she can see evidence of new growth—that the box balls may have been scorched by the pee of a visiting dog (or even a fox doing his nocturnal rounds), who seem to find 'sentry' plants as irresistible as lamp posts. The plants will continue to recover, slowly—as long as the visitations do not continue.

5. Finally, there is the nastiest option: box blight. There are two fungal diseases that affect box, and Heidi will have to take a close look at the foliage to see if she can spot signs of them. The pinkish spores of the lesser of the two evils, *Volutella buxi*, appear on the backs of the leaves and are spread (as is hollyhock rust) via rain splashing them up from the soil. By snipping out the affected branches, clearing up fallen leaves and spraying with a systemic fungicide, this might be controllable—given that the plants are in pots rather than in the ground. The other—*Cylindrocladium buxicola*—showing first as black

spots on the leaves, is virtually unstoppable and has been known to wipe out whole hedges. If after careful inspection Heidi suspects that her plants are diseased, I think she should go back to the nursery from which she bought them, taking the plants with her. I hope she kept her receipt.

GARDENERS' MUMBO JUMBO

This is a plea for simplicity. Why don't garden writers use the accepted common name of plants and trees as well as the scientific name? Not all of us have gardening reference books to help us translate **Trachelospermum jasminoides,** *for example, into understandable English, even if we learnt Latin at school. My guess is that this is a type of jasmine—am I right?*
N G, Northwich, Cheshire

I really do try to put in common names as often as I can, as I am acutely aware (having taught basic gardening to complete beginners) of how off-putting and irritating all the Latin can be. However, I feel I must give you just a little insight as to why it is hard to be straightforward all the time...

Centuries ago, in order to make plant classification easier for themselves, botanists gave plants Latin names and put them into various categories or 'families', membership of which depended on all sorts of botanical details of which many normal, even experienced gardeners are largely ignorant. Latin was quite naturally used (along with some Greek) since they were the universal languages of learning. No one since has come up with a system that is anything like as good.

So no, *Trachelospermum jasminoides* is not jasmine, and doesn't even belong to the same family as jasmine. The '-oides' on the end of the name is there to indicate that it is 'jasmine-like', and is one of numerous suffixes that appear on the end of the names of plants that superficially, but not botanically, resemble others.

I have discovered that trachelospermum does have an 'English' (or more probably, American) name—confederate jasmine or star jasmine—which I have never seen used. However, it is sometimes referred to as evergreen jasmine, and in fact there are several similar varieties (*T. asiaticum*, with smaller leaves, being one), so, you see, all parts of a plant name are crucial, not just the first part.

Garden writers will generally err heavily on the side of caution when naming plants. They know that as soon as they start cutting corners and simplifying things for their readers, a dozen hard-nosed botanists will jump out from behind a pile of dusty books and have a go at them—and change the names of a few plants into the bargain, just in order to really put the cat among the pigeons. Do you begin to see the problem?

A PROBLEM WITH PILES?

Bridget and Richard don't like mulch-cutting their grass (see May, page 59) because it makes a mess that inevitably gets walked into their house. They are, therefore, tearing their hair out about the massive piles of outwardly crusty, inwardly sludgy grass clippings that accumulate as a result of conventionally mowing their two and a half acre garden. What can they do with these piles, they ask? They must be usable in some way to benefit their veg garden—or roses—or something, surely?

I have used cloddy compost like this to mulch my raspberries each spring. It could also be useful in this half-rotted state plonked on top of empty veg beds as an organic winter duvet. The action of worms, weather and blackbirds will spread it around and break it down further, and it can then be dug into the soil in the spring. How about spreading it around hedge-bottoms, or under evergreen shrubs where it can't be seen?

Next summer, perhaps they could do more to help the grass clippings to rot down faster and more effectively—by mixing them with shredded paper, straw or cardboard, and/or using one of the compost activators made specifically for the purpose such as Biotal Compost Maker.

SEAWEED FOR THE GARDEN

Having previously fed the soil in my London garden with home-made compost, I am currently digging horse manure into the stony soil in my new garden so that I can start to

220

plant next spring. I would also like to make use of seaweed as a soil improver—my garden is five minutes from the beach. Can it be used 'neat' or should it be mixed with other organic matter? Does it need to be washed? I would appreciate any information.
Brian, Christchurch, Dorset

Seaweed has roughly the same nitrogen, phosphate and potassium levels as horse manure, together with various minerals and trace elements—it has been used by coastal farmers and gardeners for centuries. You should concentrate on collecting fresh seaweed that has been recently washed up at or below the tide line. Wet, fresh seaweed has, surprisingly enough, a far lower salt content than the smelly, crisp stuff that has been sitting around drying on the beach during the summer.

Washing seaweed before using it is not really necessary. This is a good time of year to collect and use it, and it can be dug directly into the soil where it will rot down during the winter. Or you can collect it and chop it up slightly and incorporate it into an ordinary compost heap, much as you would with any ordinary garden waste materials. I would not, however, plan on stacking it up and storing it on its own, as it will inevitably get rather malodorous, as you can imagine.

DISAPPOINTING PANSIES

Despondent Jane from Hatton in Warwickshire asks whether it is really worth growing pansies in baskets and containers during the winter. By March, she says, hers are lanky, washed out and miserable. I do understand her plight. The trouble is, we have rather high expectations of these distinctly temperamental 'winter-flowering' pansies. They seem to have a natural tendency to sulk and go sick in periods of damp, sunless weather—of which we have plenty—and be extraordinarily likely, I find, to succumb to a rather nasty fungal leaf spot by the end of the winter, which stunts their growth and can ultimately kill them. Depending on how bad hers are, Jane could trim all the straggly, barely flowering shoots right back now, give the plants a liquid feed and spray them with a systemic fungicide such as Systhane—which just might knock the leaf spot on the head and get things going again for one last little flourish before she chucks them out and replaces them with some summer stuff in a few weeks' time. In future years, it may be worth spraying them with a fungicide as a preventative measure in the middle of the winter.

BULB EATERS

Do you have any ideas as to what is tunnelling into the soil and eating my carefully planted bulbs? Could it be mice? Alliums and tulips are all disappearing. Last year tulips came up and

*keeled over when in flower. On investigation I
discovered that there were no bulbs attached to
the stems.*
Rosie, by email

You don't give me much information about
the nature of your garden, but my first
thought is that the damage is too devastating
to be the work of mice, because they tend to
operate above ground and you say the
perpetrator of all this havoc is a tunneller. I
think it is more likely to be a plague of voles.
They form substantial underground colonies,
burrowing and tunnelling in dry grassy banks
and in undisturbed compost heaps, doing all
manner of damage to roots and bulbs on
which they feed. Vole populations fluctuate
depending on the mildness or otherwise of
our winters. Baiting and trapping them is
hard—but I understand from various readers
that they have a fondness for peanut butter.
Their major natural predators are cats and
owls, and when the subject of vole damage
was aired previously, another reader
informed me that his solution was to put a tall
stout post in the ground near the site of his
vole colony for owls to sit on at night. It
worked apparently.

CORDYLINES

*I have two 6ft (1.8m) tall cordylines that must
now be about 15 years old, one with green
leaves, one with red, growing in 24in (60cm)
tubs. I wrap them in fleece in the winter to*

protect them from wind. Would they be better
planted out in the ground? The red-leaved one
now has three small 'babies' growing from its
base. Can I remove them and grow them on as
new plants?
Christine, by email

Spiky *Cordyline australis* became really
popular around 10 or so years ago, and I
suspect there must now be a lot of middle-
aged specimens hanging around in pots
looking slightly uneasy.

Although winter wind and frost protection
will always be an issue here, cordylines are
hardier than you might suppose, and certainly
in the south of the UK it is possible to grow
them in the ground where, if anything, their
roots will be more protected than they would
be in a pot. In addition to the usual fleece
protection for the top (and possibly bubble
wrap for potted specimens), you can bunch
the outer leaves up and tie them together
loosely to give extra protection to the central
spike. During mild spells the cover can be
removed and any nestling earwigs or
catatonic snails should be shooed out.

As for the babies, if they are coming from
the base of the plant, they can be carefully cut
away with a little bit of the root, potted on
into sandy compost and kept indoors for the
coming winter (a cold bedroom would be
ideal). Chances of success: I'd say about
50/50.

Incidentally, the branched specimens of
cordyline that you see in warmer climates are

the result of the plants flowering. Once they start to flower, the stems produce extra side shoots and the plants change completely in character as a result.

PRUNING PASSION FLOWERS

I have a passion flower (Passiflora caerulea) which this year has gone mad by growing about 15ft (4.5m) in one season. I am tidying up the garden for the winter and would like to know if I should treat it the same way as a climbing rose by pruning all but the main arterial growth. Since I live in the south-west, there is little fear that the plant will be frosted.
John, Falmouth, Cornwall

This passion flower, with its strange, intricate flowers and pendulous (unpalatable) orange fruit, is a rampant beast and most probably, in your neck of the woods, quite frost-hardy. It is also a somewhat disorganised climber, using its tendrils to scramble all over the place quite uncontrollably. In my experience it does not—unlike climbing roses or ornamental vines, for example—make an easily disciplined woody framework to which you can prune back each year. So I would lop this climber back by at least half now, which will enable you to tidy up the garden more easily. Even though you say your garden is sheltered, instinctively I feel it would be tempting providence to cut the entire plant back to the ground just before winter. Return to the plant in March, however, and reduce the stuff you left behind as winter protection. Bear in mind that your plant will put on between 10–15ft (3–4.5m) of messy, flowery growth every year from now on, principally from the point at which it is cut, and that young, new shoots coming from the base of the plant will be far more pleasing to look at than growth produced off the previous year's stems.

HYPERICUM LOWDOWN

Emailer M A wonders if a hitherto unpruned vast *Hypericum* 'Hidcote' at the back of a mixed border will come to any harm if it is cut right down now to make room for more perennials. It would be better to wait till spring before cutting this shrub to the quick, and it should not be forgotten that it will put out about 4ft (1.2m) of growth in all directions next season before flowering. My advice is to cut it back by about half now, and complete the job next spring. And keep any new perennials at least 4ft (1.2m) away.

JAPANESE ENEMIES

A friend has offered me some white Japanese anemones, of which he has a large and beautiful colony. I have tried in the past to transplant a small clump to my garden and failed. When and how should I try again? Do they need any special treatment?
Jane, Leicestershire

Japanese anemones are as tough as old boots,

admirably shade and drought tolerant and will spread like wildfire. Transplanting and establishing them, however, can be tricky, as you have found out, because they have enormously deep and brittle roots. If you are really determined to have these lovely things in your garden—and to my mind they almost qualify as an official garden hooligan—then you should dig up several pieces now with as much root intact as possible and pot them up separately (reuse tall black plastic pots if you have some, and a soil-based compost such as John Innes No 2) in the hope that at least some of them will survive. Those that show signs of life early in the spring should be nurtured in their pots until early next autumn, at which time they can be carefully de-potted and planted with a fistful of bonemeal where you want them to grow. They may need watering for the first year. Do take care where you site them. These beasts are capable of forcing their way up between paving stones once they get going, and produce an ocean of thick foliage in mid-summer before they flower that can endanger other less robust plants.

SYCAMORE SPOTS

Maggie wonders whether she should burn all the fallen leaves from her large sycamore tree each year, since they are clearly diseased (they are covered in large black spots). She is concerned that if she just adds them to her leaf heaps the disease will inevitably spread to her two small ornamental acers, which belong to the same plant family as the sycamore. I suspect that there is little point in worrying about this extremely common fungal disease (called acer tar spot) which attacks sycamores but actually does no harm to them. In theory it could spread to the ornamental acers, but if it hasn't already done so it may be her tree has a strain of the disease that is specific to sycamores.

AND THEN, ON OCCASIONS, I JUST HAVE TO DEFEND MYSELF AGAINST THE BARBS...

I am shocked that you encourage irresponsible attitudes to brambles. These are native plants that grow naturally in scrub and woodland—precursors to hedgerows. To remove them is simply destroying Britain's biodiversity. Shame on you.
David, by email

I am reluctant to take issue with readers, but I feel I must answer your criticism (of which the above is just a précis) of my stance on brambles in gardens. Having been for many years the custodian of a large country garden adjoining unkempt woodland and farmland, I found it totally unrealistic to embrace brambles as an acceptable garden plant. I am sure my experience is typical. Where possible I used to train brambles along my boundary hedges and I harvested the fruit—in partnership with the large local bird population, which I also encouraged by providing innumerable undisturbed nesting sites as well as additional winter food. But in the cultivated and more formal areas of the garden the brambles (which spread rapidly out of the hedges, burying their shoot tips and making new roots and independent plants), were intolerably invasive, spread additionally of course by seed, via the very birds with which I shared the fruit.

I try to promote and encourage a thoughtful, careful attitude to the use of chemicals and the protection of wildlife, but frequently find myself under attack from those who would protect and preserve every living thing on the planet. I would point out that if we gardeners were to do as they wish, our gardens would be ugly places and our precious plants overwhelmed by an ocean of bindweed, couch grass, knotweed, bramble and ground elder—none of which seem to be put off their stroke to any helpful degree by mildew or rust, or by attacks from insects, slugs, rabbits or deer.

POTTED BAY TREES

As a wedding gift in July my husband and I were given two potted lollipop-style bay trees in wooden tubs. We have been watering them regularly and have fed them a couple of times with a liquid feed suitable for potted plants, but we do not know much about their long-term care. We are new to gardening. Can you help?
John and Claire, by email

I would slacken off on the feeding now that the growing season is over and keep their compost just moist for the winter. You may be pleased to learn that bay is relatively trouble free. There is an unpleasant, disfiguring pest called bay sucker that attacks the leaves occasionally. The tell-tale signs are thickening and curving-over of the edges of the leaves, under which the nymphs hide in a white, woolly, waxy covering. You can spray with an insecticide in spring (you will need to do it twice) or try to keep control of things with a bit of judicious pruning. Your little trees will need to be pruned anyway to keep them compact and neat. This should be done once growth has really got under way in spring and again somewhere around July or August if the bushes are very vigorous. Snip out whole shoot tips with secateurs or kitchen scissors to maintain the shape—don't use shears since the cut leaves can look unsightly. Dry some of the leaves (just hang them up) for cooking. Frequently trimmed bay lollipops are unlikely to flower much, if at all—a shame really, since the little flower clusters are rather attractive in a low-key way, and have a delicate scent. The trees will eventually need to be re-potted, but not for a year to two.

Bay trees are quite hardy if kept in sheltered doorways (as they most often are) in urban and suburban gardens. However, they could suffer from scorched leaves if exposed to harsh frosty wind, and you may find it necessary to cover their tops temporarily. Finally, if the pots are placed hard against a wall with limited light, turn them occasionally and even swap them over, to encourage even growth.

ON HEDGEHOGS

Elizabeth wonders whether she should put out food for hedgehogs to encourage them into her garden, and asks if there are any DISadvantages of having them around. I know of no glaringly obvious ones, and love to see them bundling around my own garden from time to time, although they do not completely solve my slug and snail problem as Elizabeth's sister claims they do in hers.

Several thoughts spring to mind here: hedgehogs like gardens with scruffy, unkempt corners where they can shamble around and hide in winter—so to encourage them you have to learn to be a bit untidy. I understand we shouldn't really feed hedgehogs (particularly bread and milk) because it is not good for them. However (and I suppose on reflection this could be seen as a disadvantage of having them around), hedgehogs can have terrible fleas which can easily be picked up by household pets...

...A PRICKLY ISSUE

Not all hedgehogs have fleas, I am assured by several readers, and anyway fleas are host-specific and therefore would not cause a problem on household pets. (I know all this, but I beg to differ—look at any dog's muzzle when they have been messing with a hedgehog. Fleas will temporarily hop on board any passing animal, much as cat and dog fleas can temporarily hop on board—and maybe bite—us.) Apparently I showed myself to be 'prejudiced' against hedgehogs. Actually, careful readers will have observed that I love them and keep a deliberately scruffy garden in order to provide them with places to hang out. Now calm down and stow your prickles, everyone.

WINTER

December

PROPER-GATION

'You can't call yourself a proper gardener unless you have a greenhouse.' This feather-ruffling statement made by a gardening friend (flushed with a pretty justified sense of achievement, having sown over a hundred sweet peas in Rootrainers in her newly refurbished glorious Edwardian glasshouse), gave me food for thought. I certainly regarded myself as a 'proper' gardener long before I got my little greenhouse. So I find myself writing defensively for all those who have neither the space—nor the considerable time needed—to do greenhousey stuff on anything but the smallest scale. 'Proper' gardeners everywhere deftly raise annuals from seed, take softwood cuttings in algae-filled jars that look like dippings from a primordial swamp, chit potatoes and overwinter assorted tender perennials with little more than a garage or spare bedroom windowsill to play with. A few may have a handy frost-free glazed porch, of course, but even a conservatory is not necessarily an ideal horticultural playground. It may provide much-needed light, but may well be too hot and dry and quickly get stuffed with tender 'conservatory' plants, smart furniture—and people.

One reader writes that she propagates basil by shoving shoots from a supermarket pot into a jar of water, waiting for roots to sprout before gently transferring them into pots of compost. This 'primordial swamp' method of propagation is ideal for beginners with the enthusiasm to experiment with anything soft stemmed—carefully removing lower leaves minimises the 'swamp' aspect—to see what works and what doesn't. The slightly more sophisticated may like to try the hormone-rooting-gel pots, which have a high success rate with semi-hardwood cuttings such as argyranthemums and fuchsias as well.

Growing annuals from seed in spring is an altogether more complex kettle of fish for the spatially challenged. Firstly, wait. Do not sow seeds until quite late in the spring—in order to avoid having to keep small seedlings hanging around, becoming more and more gangly from lack of light, before the weather has warmed up sufficiently to put them out in the garden. However late you sow, the plants seem quite surprisingly to 'catch up'.

Secondly, it pays only to grow a little of any one thing—a single germinated pot-full (rather than a seed tray-full) of seeds will yield, ultimately, enough young plants for a goodly patch of colour in a small garden. Stick to manageable-sized seeds. Those of nicotiana, for example, are like dust—extremely hard to deal with, even when mixed with sand. After germination, keep the strongest five or so seedlings in each batch to eventually pot on, and ditch the rest. Thirdly, drench your seedlings and their compost with a fungicide such as Cheshunt compound (which can be mixed up in very small quantities), to avoid tragic 'damping off' (seedlings collapsing soon after germination). Fourthly, seedlings will frizzle up in harsh, direct sunshine. Give them a situation that is as light and

236

bright as possible and turn the pots daily.

Growing things on a windowsill is made easier by using narrow, sill-shaped, clear-lidded propagators, and I have also used tall fibre grow-tubes (good for sweet peas), shoehorning a few tubes together into a large black plastic plant pot so that they stay damp and can be moved around easily. Cling film makes temporary covers to keep germinating seeds (or little cuttings) moist, or you can rig up polybag/wire hoop/rubber band constructions that used to be called, rather grandly, Wisley cloches. None of this is easy or ideal, but in a small way you can get 'proper' results.

TIME TO SIT ON YOUR HANDS...

Impatient readers, all novice rose growers, have written asking if it is OK to prune them now. I am assuming they are asking for my opinion rather than for official permission, although sometimes I wonder, from the tone of your communications, if I am perceived as some appalling, grumpy old garden dragon.

Frustrating though it may be, I feel this is a little early to be thinking about pruning roses. The problem is that, in the warmer counties at least, roses seem very reluctant to go into winter dormancy—which is when the work is best carried out. Pruning too soon can in fact encourage a late flush of growth, which is then vulnerable to the frosts that normally don't really hit us hard until after Christmas. So personally, I plan a session for late January/early February (see pages 268–9). Northerners and those with exposed gardens tend to leave it later still. As long as it is all done by the end of March, which is when roses start to stir their stumps again, all will be well.

Emailer Terry has a three-year-old rambler, 'Wedding Day', that desperately needs 'sorting out'—and we can guess what he has in mind, can't we? It's growing on a fence, he says, with great big thorny shoots waving about all over the place. He wants to cut them all off, while Mrs Terry says they should be tied down to the fence.

Compromise, dear people, compromise. Ramblers produce their best flowers on younger wood. If Terry has his wicked way and cuts all the new shoots off each year, the rose will always flower badly. If Mrs Terry has hers, the rose will become an almighty mess and the fence will most probably, in due course, collapse. The answer is that some of the oldest shoots (they will be brownish, not bright green) should be snipped out, bit by bit, right down to ground level, bringing with it, of course, much of the rose's vast top growth as well. Then one or two, or maybe three or four, of the remaining over-long bright green shoots should be tied in to the fence and the remainder cut severely. (You can do this kind of 'emergency' work in summer too, as I've explained in 'Rambling On and On', page 135.) So Terry can do some very limited first aid on the rambler right now (doubtless under careful supervision) to stop the long shoots blowing about and snagging the washing. But the main job should be done in a few weeks' time. After which Mr and Mrs Terry can argue about what to do next, because this rose is very definitely in the wrong place. Big ramblers belong up trees. End of story.

MOSSY BORDERS

Despite having free-draining sandy soil Linda's borders in Knutsford, Cheshire, are covered in a thick carpet of moss. If she tries to scrape it off and dispose of it, she says, she loses a lot of the soil beneath it. If she forks it over and trowels it in will this make the problem worse, she asks? And how should she dispose of all that moss? If she puts it on her compost heap (which is a fairly slow-acting cold one) will it be killed? Or will she end up spreading moss around when she uses the compost on the garden next year?

I can say from experience, having lived for the past decade in the High Weald, with its clean damp air and slightly acid soil—moss heaven, in fact—that if your garden is basically mossy, then you will always have a problem with it. It doesn't just thrive in the damp and in the shade; it can spread all over the place.

It sounds to me as if Linda's borders are going from year to year virtually undisturbed, and this could be largely why such a thick blanket of moss has covered the soil. I find that moss can to a great extent be put off its stroke by regular twiddling-about of the soil. This doesn't need to be deep, back-breaking digging and soil-turning; indeed such violent activity is unnecessary and inappropriate in a planted-up area. But each spring I weed, I fiddle the previous year's mulch into the soil around the established plants (thereby constantly improving it) with the aid of my beloved long-handled fork with its tiny 'head', before I apply more organic stuff. In the 'off' season there

239

is always a certain amount of moving of plants to be done, dividing and replanting and so on, which means that the moss can rarely get a foothold. So, although it may be of no comfort to Linda—and it is probably very bossy of me to say so: I think she needs to get out there and do more gardening if she wants to get the upper hand where the moss is concerned.

To answer the question about moss in compost heaps: never the twain should meet. Moss absolutely does not die. It goes moribund and brown when dry, which is why mossy lawns that look fine in the winter look so dire in the summer—but will always perk up again once conditions suit it. So it goes without saying that all the scarifyings and rakings from mossy lawns should definitely be binned.

STRANGE GOINGS-ON IN THE TREES

Dave from Frampton Cotterell is concerned about the 'greenish mildew-like fungus' that covers the branches and trunks of his magnolia, azaleas and apple trees, and has been trying to get rid of it. This sounds like algae—the same green film that covers shady steps, paving stones and garden furniture during the winter months in mild damp weather. Like witches' brooms (the twiggy masses that also appear in silver birch trees), these algal growths are harmless. They are spread by spores that are constantly in the air, making them virtually impossible to eradicate or even control, if the conditions suit them. Dave should try to turn a blind eye, I feel. It will be less obvious once the trees are in leaf. Certain trees do benefit aesthetically from a clean-up, however. I wash my white-barked birch (*Betula utilis* var. *jacquemontii*) each winter around this time with Biotal Algae and Mould Stain Cleaner (from garden centres in dilute or concentrate form), which is plant, pet and pond-life friendly and also works on steps, paving stones and furniture.

LICHEN OR NOT?

It would seem to be lichen time of year again. Once the leaves are well and truly down and the bare bones of our gardens are visible again, readers start to get alarmed about yellow and grey/green dry 'growths' of various types on their trees and bushes. Frilly grey patches of lichen on a damson tree are worrying R W from Malvern; Nancy from Bessels Green in Kent has noticed that lichen has now spread from her old azaleas on to a *Magnolia stellata* and a witch hazel; while Mrs C from Northamptonshire sent me a photograph of bright yellow lichen coating the stems of her hibiscus. Is there a treatment that will get rid of the unsightly stuff, they ask?

Lichens are composite organisms—in unscientific terms they are a cross between algae and fungi—that proliferate via airborne spores and grow particularly well in places where the air is damp and clean. They tend to grow on woody plants that are themselves growing extremely slowly, but they actually do no harm to their hosts. There is no 'treatment' that will control the growth of lichen but, depending on where it is growing, you can often, with a bit of sensible pruning, remove some of the oldest, worst affected shoots.

241

You should also kick-start the growth of all slow-growing trees and shrubs, grubbing out any throttling weeds or grass from around their feet and applying an appropriate fertiliser and a good, foody mulch such as compost or leaf mould in the spring.

TENDER BOUGAINVILLEAS

Claire in London and others are reluctant to believe their bougainvilleas that did so well this year are not hardy and seem determined to leave them outside for the winter. If they do they are bound to be disappointed. Bougainvilleas must be kept frost free in winter and will almost certainly lose their leaves and be severely retarded if they are kept at a temperature of less than 10°C (50°F). Naturally, having written this with total confidence, I half expect some jammy smarty-pants who has a positive furnace of a garden somewhere in Bournemouth to write in and make a liar of me.

(PS—He did.)

HARDY AND NOT SO HARDY CYCLAMEN

J F from Letchworth asks about the identity of the little pink and sometimes white cyclamen she has seen growing in gardens recently. Are they a special hardy kind, or are they just last year's little potted winter cyclamen that people have put outside?

The cyclamen she has seen are *Cyclamen hederifolium*; small patterned leaves are produced as the flowers fade, and they then become most attractive, extremely shade-tolerant foliage ground cover for several months. There is a spring-flowering species that is similar, *C. coum*. They get going best, I have found, if bought in small pots of gritty soil.

Both these little hardy cyclamen will self-seed freely and eventually form small colonies—in fact Christine's are already on their way to doing so. She wrote to ask what she should do with the small, corm-like blobs on the end of spiralled stems that she has found on her now-established plants. These are the seedpods and are best left just to do their own thing.

The winter cyclamen that are starting to appear in florists' shops are not hardy, being hybrids of *C. persicum*—although they do tolerate very low temperatures outside and, if dried off after flowering, will just about go from year to year, if you are lucky and manage to keep vine weevils away from them.

STORING MANURE

As an ex-townie, I have never before had the luxury of free horse manure. Books all say it should be 'well-rotted', but never give details. Do I: a) leave it in its original plastic bags, b) empty it out and cover it, or c) empty it out and leave it uncovered?
Dr C, Wickham Bishops, Essex

First, do the smell tests: really well-rotted manure should be more or less pong-free. If yours isn't, I would leave it in the bags for a while longer—it will go on rotting in there quite happily, as long as the bags are pretty much sealed up. Another option is to mix your manure into an existing compost heap, which will help to speed up the rotting considerably. Whatever you do, don't just leave it in a pile uncovered, since any useful heat will dissipate and the winter rain will wash some of the goodness out of it.

Free horse manure that is not well rotted, as well as being too 'strong' for safe contact with plant roots and shoots, potentially carries loads of weed/grass seed. So the longer it rots in its nice, steaming, original farmyard heap the better. If you have to go to bag it up yourself (this is often part of the deal), try to avoid just taking the fresh unrotted stuff from the top of the pile. Equally hazardous can be old muck heaps that have been sitting around in the corner of a field for years. The top layer may be contaminated with thistle or nettle seeds. Moral: dig deeply.

ORNAMENTAL GRASS QUERIES

I have so far fought shy of planting grasses in my borders because they can look messy. This year I was persuaded to plant two, however—a grey bristly one, helictotrichon, and a variegated taller miscanthus. What should I be doing with them now? I hope I haven't introduced a couple of thugs.
Julia, Durham

Fear not, you have chosen a couple of 'safe'

grasses. Neither of these two is a manic self-seeder in the style of annual grasses such as the lovely barley look-alike *Hordeum jubatum* (squirrel tail grass) or some of the perennial stipas such as fluffy *S. tenuissima* and *S. arundinacea* (pheasant's tail grass, now renamed *Anemanthele lessoniana*), all of which can colonise far too fast for comfort. Nor will these grasses run amok, almost couch-grass style, like *Phalaris arundinacea* var. *picta* (gardener's garters).

The *Helictotrichon sempervirens* (blue oat grass) needs little attention. It is a truly evergreen (or ever-grey) grass and will look pretty good throughout the winter (especially with frost on it), producing fresh growth and pale flower spikelets early next summer without dying off. Simply run your fingers up through the clump at intervals (now, and again in the spring). You will be surprised to find how much beige, dry dead stuff you will be able to remove without effort, which will smarten up the plant a lot. (A good way of tidying up stipas too.) In my experience, however, this grass does not stay lovely for ever, and may burn itself out and need replacing after a couple of years.

Miscanthus sinensis 'Variegatus' is only marginally trickier. It is probably looking really good now but by mid-winter will have become extremely ratty-looking and you will be itching to cut it down. The later in the winter you leave it, the more careful you have to be not to sever the small forest of next year's new shoots that start to grow—albeit slowly—from quite early in the spring. If in doubt, leave several inches of the old growth intact.

OVERWINTERING CHOCOLATE COSMOS

Jenny asks what she should do with her chocolate cosmos (*Cosmos atrosanguineus*) for the winter. She acquired one that performed somewhat disappointingly last summer. However, it is 'still just alive', planted in a sunny part of her garden in Wiltshire and although she knows it is tender, she wants to try to keep it going. Is it better to mulch it heavily and leave it alone, or dig it up and overwinter it indoors?

Despite its frequently wimpish and disappointing performance, together with the fact that its young foliage is regarded as caviar by slugs and snails, and its small, dark, slightly dahlia-like flowers exude only the merest whiff of our favourite indulgence, chocolate cosmos seems to have become sensationally popular over the past few years. As a native of Mexico (and now thought to be extinct in the wild), it seems to hate spending the winter in our cold, wet soil and I am surprised that it is sold as a garden perennial. I feel Jenny's best bet would be to lift her plant from the ground and pot up the fairly delicate tuberous root into some fresh, dry compost, store the pot in a frost-free place for the winter and keep her fingers firmly crossed. It will be infuriatingly late to show signs of growth next spring, and it may well do better anyway if kept in a pot next summer rather than returned to the ground.

Emailer Yvonne clearly has more luck, skill and

determination than most. Her three plants were 'prolific' last summer and she wants to propagate from them to give plants away to friends (now that's what I call just plain bragging). I understand that the best way to propagate this plant is to divide the tubers carefully in spring.

BIRD CALL

Faye and Peter ask if there is anything they can put in their garden bird bath that will stop the water freezing without harming either the birds or the bird bath. Faye thought a drop of gin might do the trick but then thought better of it. Like many (most, I would like to think) gardeners, I greatly appreciate my feathered garden visitors and, as we are encouraged to do, I now feed them all the year round. To encourage all comers I put out an assortment of different types of food. Seed tubes containing peanuts and sunflower hearts, bought as cheaply as possible in bulk and stored in lidded bins in my garage, hang off a high bird table placed close to trees and hedges. These provide cover and perching places (in which, among others, gold and green finches, various tits and even nuthatches queue for 'their turn'), but I make sure there is no thick evergreen growth at ground level near the table in which the one or two malevolent-looking local moggies can lie in wait. Elsewhere outside, on the ground close to my French windows, I put out different food entirely—mostly apples, chopped or grated scraps of old cheese or cheap porridge oats slightly moistened with vegetable oil (I mix this up in big batches). My ground-feeding birds, among them beady-eyed blackbirds, dunnocks and a pair of softly twittering robins, have become incredibly tame and stay close to me while I am at work in the garden or simply hang around in the bushes waiting for my appearance. Gangs of jeering, clattering starlings flock down from the oak tree to splash around the edge of the pond and demolish all available food in seconds while disapproving collar doves sit on the garage roof and pass judgement on the state of my unkempt garden (…how ghaaastly, how ghaaastly…). It is a wonder I get any writing done at all.

But back to Faye and Peter's query. Clean, fresh water is extremely important for birds all year round, and not just for drinking. Splashing in it helps to control parasites and generally keep feathers in good condition—vital if birds are to stay in fine fettle and weather the weather, so to speak. There is a totally natural product available that will keep bird baths and drinking stations ice free without harming them. It is sold under the Just Green label and helpfully called Ice Free for Bird Baths. Garden bird care is now big business and it pays to shop around for good deals on winter staples such as fat balls and also buy bulk bags of seeds and seed mixtures. Remember that the more varied the diet you provide, the greater will be the diversity of your feathered visitors.

PROTECTING BANANAS

We have two potted banana plants (Musa lasiocarpa) that we grew this year from cuttings from last year's plants. We would like to keep these over the winter but have nowhere

indoors to house them. What should we do to
protect them outside?
Sheila, by email

I am reliably informed that this variety is
similarly (i.e. barely) hardy in this country to
the more commonly grown *M. basjoo* and will
need fairly careful winter protection as you
suspect. The best way to protect plants that
are in the ground is to stand a terracotta
chimney pot or section(s) of terracotta flue
liner (from builders' suppliers) over the 2ft
(60cm) remains of the cut-down stems before
winter really arrives, and fill in around the
stems with straw, aiming to achieve about a
4in (10cm) layer all around them. An old
ridge tile will make a suitable roof to keep
out the worst of the winter wet. The
protection should be removed fairly smartly
around March, and even if the new leaves get
nipped by subsequent rogue frosts, the plant
will rally later in the spring and grow rapidly
thereafter.

In your case, perhaps the best thing to do
would be to sink the pots into the soil in a
sheltered spot in the garden and do as
described above. The plants will have the
added protection of the surrounding soil
(which in really cold weather is likely to stay
warmer than the air above ground) and can
be lifted in March when the upper protection
is removed.

WISE WORDS ON DETERRING DEER

Here are readers' top tips for stopping them feasting on garden plants. Alison in Cornwall uses black plastic deer protection netting for individual roses and camellias. She also drapes finer, lightweight black butterfly netting over her flowerbeds—it's almost invisible, and it seems to do the trick, she says.

Rather than putting up barriers, Sue sprays her plants with a vile potion. She mixes up 4 cloves of garlic, 1 raw egg, 1 cup of milk and a gallon of water. Four days later the concoction can be strained into a garden sprayer. Vulnerable plants should be dosed three times in the first week, then once a week. Sue now sprays only after rain. She says her potion is not foolproof, but she now has something akin to a garden, as do friends to whom she has passed on the recipe. Some of these were somewhat desperate, living on the edge of Ashdown Forest.

Hugh from Bardwell points out that while deer can jump normal stock fencing, they find it very hard to 'long jump', so a second fence placed about 2ft 3in (0.7m) outside the first can be an effective deterrent. Dense, thick, wide hedges, reinforced with stock netting, are also effective, according to Hugh, because deer are reluctant to jump opaque barriers. Presumably such a hedge would benefit from Sue's whiffy cocktail in its early stages of growth.

HOLLY BERRIES

Last year we had to remove a sizeable variegated holly tree from our garden because of building works. While it looked very attractive it never had any berries. We would like to replace it, possibly with a standard holly, but would prefer one that carried berries. Do we need to plant two trees, one male and one female, to achieve this?
Janet, by email

Your sadly departed tree was probably a male form, *Ilex aquifolium* 'Silver Queen'. No, I have not got it wrong; someone in the holly-naming department was clearly having a bit of fun, since the female variegated holly is called 'Golden King'.

If there are other holly trees or hedges in or around your garden that would pollinate it, you could therefore plant a 'Golden King', and you would be sure of getting berries from it. However, if you feel that there is some doubt about this, you could go for one of the hollies that are conveniently self-fertile and do the whole job all by themselves. The most well-known variety is *Ilex aquifolium* 'J. C. van Tol' (perhaps the 'J.C.' stands for 'jolly confused'), and the variegated form, quite easy to find in garden centres and often grown as a standard, called 'Golden van Tol'.

A TALE OF TWO LAWNS

Michelle describes herself as a keen gardener and a desperate mother-in-law. Five weeks ago her son-in-law treated the lawn in his newly acquired, immaculate garden with weed and feed. He is devastated that the bare patches created by the 'weed' bit of the treatment have not yet disappeared. All instructions were followed exactly, she says. Have I any advice?

Oh dear. I can well imagine the level of hair-tearing that is going on here. Michelle's son-in-law may well have followed the instructions to the letter, but he made one vital mistake: this is really the wrong time of year to be weeding and feeding a lawn. He should have waited until everything was actively growing next spring; when the areas of dead weed would have rapidly been overrun by the newly invigorated grass and the whole process of recovery would naturally be very swift.

On no account should panic ruin the entire family's Christmas, however. Nor should son-in-law scurry around desperately trying to repair the patches now. He should take some kind of comfort from the realisation that this lawn was clearly absolutely riddled with weed and yet the garden still looked 'immaculate'. This should teach him an extremely useful lesson for the future. Grass has an amazing way of regenerating all by itself and the bald patches will start to repair themselves quite quickly in early March, if not before. If still worried by April, when grass really kicks off, s-i-l can gently over-seed the worst areas.

Jack from Basingstoke dug up and re-seeded

two patches of lawn earlier in the year. Both areas have now 'settled' and sunk and the joins between the old untouched area and the newly seeded ones are very much in evidence. What should he do? Lower the level of the old grass, or raise the level of the new grass? Without seeing the areas in question, I can only advise in fairly general terms. However, I am certain this is just one version of a very common problem.

I strongly suspect that the subsidence of this new area is too great to be dealt with by simply adding top dressing (a sandy-soil mixture) to bring the level up. Adding anything other than the thinnest layer of top dressing to a patch of grass may kill it off. I think the best course of action, if the grass is now well established, might be to very carefully slice off the newly made 'turf' layer, re-compact the soil that was beneath and add to it substantially to bring the level up before putting the turf gently back. This will probably be more successful than removing the turf in the old areas and taking away soil to reduce it to the height of the new lumpy areas.

SCRUFFY WINTER IRISES

Sheila from Wigtownshire has been enjoying the usual generous crop of gorgeous pale lilac flowers from her *Iris unguicularis*. However, after many years, she says, the foliage lets the side down and is rather scruffy. She asks if she should cut it all down. This is a plant that hates shocks and I tend to have a go at my own patch a couple of times a year, just pulling out or snipping off with kitchen scissors all the old brown leaves. The heavenly short-lived flowers are best picked and enjoyed indoors—that way you can almost ignore the plant's innate messiness.

MISTLETOE MISERY

John of Cheltenham is being unseasonably bah humbug about a surfeit of what he calls a 'parasitic nuisance'—mistletoe in his garden. Mistletoe is not in fact a parasitic plant and will not harm his numerous fruit trees. If he simply can't be doing with all that Christmas kissy stuff, he could always chop off armfuls of the offending plant it and give it away to those who can.

....And finally,
No, I am sorry Mrs D, I will not 'say a word in favour of Japanese knotweed'. I would get lynched.

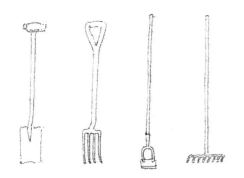

January

A SEASONALLY AFFECTED GARDENER

I have a shocking confession to make, but one with which I am sure some readers may empathise. For a month or so in winter, once the autumn colours have lost their vibrancy and the damp days close in, I fall seriously out of love with my garden, and with gardening in general. When leaden skies open, I sit in my little office racking my brains over your assorted queries and problems and can barely bring myself to look out through the rain-streaked windows. Even on better days, a pessimistic inertia overwhelms me as I tramp every soggy inch of the place, looking at everything, seeing little, achieving less, pretending that I have no time to get stuck into any meaningful jobs. It is often even too damp, too raw, to perch on a slimy bench, steaming cup in gloved hand, and just contemplate. Colonies of bittercress spring up in my collapsing borders, while branches of ratty-looking roses and threadbare honeysuckles, desperately in need of corrective surgery, wave at me in the draughty gloom. The grass literally grows beneath my feet while all around autumn leaves fall relentlessly however much I rake them up. Anything I do seems to make the garden look worse and the prospect of spring arriving gives me nightmares. I will never, ever catch up with the work, never, ever, ever... and anyway, who cares? Bloody gardening!

Something always drags me out of it, thank

goodness. Two mild breezy days blew the leaves away and dried the main lawn just enough to enable me to mow it. And then edge it. And then I cleaned the mower. Suddenly everything looked better. The next day I pruned and tied in two climbing Iceberg roses. And then I tackled the rugosas. They all instantly looked fantastic. A mistle thrush in the oak applauded loudly, tunelessly, lifting my spirits sky high. Next I barrowed up some bark chippings from the end of the garden and tarted up all the little paths in the vegetable garden. Before you could say knife, I had forked over last summer's potato patch and prepared it for this year's peas. I noticed that some salad rocket seeds cast perfunctorily under an empty cloche had all germinated. Likewise broad beans that I had presumed the mice had pinched.

The days are lengthening and I am over the worst now. I am sure I will 'catch up', although there is still a tell-tale box of unplanted tulip bulbs tucked just inside the shed to remind me of the darker days. So for what it is worth, if you can't bear the sight of your messy garden, just get out there on a bright day and do something small and constructive, anything you can manage. It will all come flooding back to you.

POINSETTIAS FOR NEXT YEAR?

I have read that there is a rather complicated procedure you have to follow to get poinsettias to perform again the following year. Since I was given a particularly good very dark red one this year, I would quite like to have a go at growing it on and making it colour up again for next

256

Christmas. What do I have to do?
Janet, by email

By all means have a go at this, but you should first realise that the poinsettias that are produced for the Christmas market are chemically dwarfed and manipulated, so you are unlikely to achieve a similarly smart, neat plant for next year.

Once your plant is past its best, you should cut it down so that the stems are no more than about 4in (10cm) tall. Keep the compost almost dry until late spring, when you should re-pot the plant and start to water it and feed it weekly. It will start to re-grow almost immediately. Remove any overcrowded new shoots as they develop, so that about four or five good ones remain. Keep the plant out of strong, hot sunshine during the summer months. The complicated bit starts in early autumn, when you will have to put a black bag over the plant's head each evening (or move it to a definitely dark cupboard or room), to ensure that it only gets 12–14 hours of daylight each day. A particularly crucial time is, apparently, the days between 10–20 October, but you should keep the bag-on-the-head bit going for a few weeks either side of these dates to be on the safe side, while at the same time keeping the plant at an even temperature.

Personally, I would find all this a fiddle too far, since the plants are so plentiful and relatively cheap to buy each year. I do, however, recommend this plant as a leafy, rather gangly-looking houseplant. It is a tender Mexican relative of our garden euphorbia (and has similarly irritant sap) and, in its natural state, is about 10ft (3m) tall. I find its reddish leaf-veins and leggy habit are actually more beguiling than its gaudy Christmas bracts.

CORSICAN BANDIT

Normally I open your squashy little packages with a certain amount of trepidation—and considerable caution. Samples of readers' problem foliage, flowers and fruit, and even vials of pond water complete with resident beasties, rarely arrive on my doormat in a good enough state to warrant a helpful or sensible comment. The only realistic answer I can give to the question 'What is wrong with this strawberry?' is that the sender was daft enough to wrap it in kitchen paper and cling film over a week ago, pop it in the post box and expect me to know...

However, the contents of a small package from R J in Gloucestershire were relatively easy to identify. They were described in the accompanying note as a sample of a plant that he and his wife had bought from Ryton Organic Garden a few years ago, recommended as an excellent subject for growing between paving slabs. At first glance the contents of the package looked like yet another disintegrating bundle of helxine, also known as Mind Your Own Business, a notorious creeping thug. However, the strong, sweet, peppery scent that wafted from the little plastic bag was unmistakably that of Corsican mint, *Mentha requienii*. R J's complaint was that the plant had now spread to a lawn in a different part of his garden, some distance from his patio, and his wife had spent many hours arduously trying to remove it by hand from both the patio and lawn with little success. I had not been previously aware that Corsican mint, a tiny-leaved shade-lover that throws up diminutive spikes of lilac-coloured flowers in summer, was such a rampant, random spreading lawn nuisance, but I suggest that if R J really wants to rid his lawn of it completely—and release poor, long-suffering Mrs R J from her life of eternal fruitless grovelling—he use a glyphosate weedkiller and eventually re-seed the lawn area affected. It seems a shame to be so harsh on this little mint, though, which must smell rather wonderful when crushed underfoot. Must we all be slaves to the ideal of the perfect greensward?

GREEN SHOOTS OF RECOVERY

Following temperatures of -10°C (14°F), a glorious, almost balmy day took us by surprise here in the south and I imagine all of us were out there opening the greenhouse doors and poking about our gardens trying to assess the extent of the havoc caused by such extraordinarily prolonged low temperatures. Then the emails started: a young mimosa tree to which the past mild winters have been kind, now sports dry, bronze-y leaves; a passion flower that has turned to rags... Are they likely to recover, their owners ask? And what should they do now?

I have to say I feared for some of my more

tender plants, including my *Euphorbia mellifera*. A treasured self-sown seedling from my old garden, it is now a buxom five-footer proudly holding court in a sunny corner. Being a sink-or-swim kind of gardener and definitely not one who rushes around at dusk with old net curtains, fleece and bubble wrap, I tend to take my chances with the weather and my shrubby euphorbias are as reliable as any thermometer. Their shoot tips, already almost swelling or, in the case of *E. characias* subsp. *wulfenii*, curled over to indicate they are only weeks away from flowering, hung limp and hideous at the first whiff of frost and remained so for days on end during deeply freezing early January, but they thankfully perked up completely as soon as daytime temperatures at last staggered above zero, and are perfectly fine.

But should truly frost-damaged plants be tidied up or cut down? Certainly, the clobbered foliage of herbaceous perennials that had hitherto forgotten it was winter—precocious alstroemerias and hollyhocks over 1ft (30cm) tall were just two examples in my garden—should be snipped cleanly away, since the slimy, matted remains can provide cover for those busy, soil-dwelling little slugs that do so much damage. But as I write more frost is forecast, and it is far too soon to let one's inner tidiness freak run riot, definitely too soon to cut back the wrecked extremities of slightly tender climbers such as passion flowers, or any shrubby plants from warmer climates—hardy fuchsias, artemisias and ceratostigmas. They will doubtless shoot out from somewhere near the base in a month or so and it is therefore best to leave all that hideous dirty-dishrag frosted top growth more or less intact until then, since it will afford some protection for those hoped-for new green shoots of recovery. But it may take even longer than that to find out whether a tender mimosa tree has survived.

THE WEEDING CAN WAIT…

My beds and borders have gradually become carpeted with weed seedlings—more than I have ever seen before. Would it be a really bad idea to just leave them until spring?
Donald, by email

There are still cold months to come and some of these weeds may be killed, others will just stop in their tracks and not budge till the weather warms up. There are a few, however, that seem to grow almost all the year round and will flower, set seed and therefore multiply at an alarming rate. One of the biggest menaces in this category is hairy bittercress, which makes tiny neat leaf rosettes and has equally tiny exploding seedpods, and is often introduced into gardens in the compost of plants bought from nurseries where maintenance is a bit haphazard. Ignore hairy bittercress at your peril, since it can form immense colonies that are hard to eradicate. Then there are perennials such as dandelions and creeping buttercup, for example, which will quickly make difficult-to-shift root systems, and are far easier to get rid of when they are small.
Unless you know you have an infestation of

something nasty like those mentioned above, I would leave things alone for now. If you use a hoe in damp conditions, many of the weedlings will just re-root in different places, and the alternative would be to weed by hand. Anyone who claims to enjoy grubbing about in muddy borders wearing knee-pads and cold wet gloves on a dreary winter day is a fibber, especially when they could be sitting indoors in their socks leafing through seed catalogues. You can tell yourself (quite rightly) that you would be doing more harm than good by compacting the soil, as well as risking all sorts of damage to about-to-emerge spring bulbs.

LEGGY SWEET PEAS

My sweet peas, sown in the autumn in big yoghurt pots, are growing alarmingly tall already. Should I plant them out in the ground I have prepared, or try to keep them going in the cold frame?
Chantal, by email

Planting them out is extremely risky and will inevitably disturb their vulnerable roots just when the worst of our winter weather might kick in. It would be hard to give their top growth adequate protection, particularly from cold wind. If I were you I would pot them on, perhaps two to a (much larger) pot, and keep them under cover. You will have to pinch out the tips of the shoots—more than once if necessary, if they continue to grow. This will make them into good, sturdy plants that will race away when you eventually do plant them out in spring.

THANK GOODNESS FOR EVERGREEN SHRUBS

Sometimes—by accident or design—we achieve plant combinations that are both easy to maintain and easy on the eye, which makes them truly satisfying. Stranded indoors by winter rain, I am grateful for the existence of a particularly pleasing bunch of evergreen shrubs that I can appreciate even from that familiar vantage point: the kitchen sink.

I like to grow evergreens in great mixed gangs—with contrasting leaf shapes, colours and textures. They make informal hedges, incredibly effective windbreaks, backdrops and climbing frames for more delicate perennial climbers. My kitchen sink group is planted as follows. The main bulk is formed by *Viburnum tinus* 'Eve Price', which is densely evergreen with pink-ish buds right now, and white unscented flowers in spring, and *Pittosporum* 'Garnettii', grown principally for its green and cream foliage with edges tinged with maroon in winter, although it bears tiny scented flowers in late spring. Most imposing of all is *Photinia* × *fraseri* 'Red Robin', an evergreen with shiny lipstick-red new shoots. Nestling under the wings of these major shrubs are smaller ones: *Pittosporum tenuifolium* 'Golden King' (a slower-growing butter-yellow-leaved variety); *Skimmia* × *confusa* 'Kew Green'; *Daphne odora* 'Aureomarginata' and *Sarcococca humilis*—all of

263

which carry scented flowers at various times in late winter and spring.

The group was planted to hide the side of a rather uninteresting brick outhouse, and to give some leafy background substance and winter interest in a shadier corner of my otherwise sunny, summer-spectacular gravel garden. The little scented shrubs considerably cheer up the path that leads to my wormery. The ground is slightly sloping, so although the soil is quite heavy it drains reasonably well (which is important for evergreens). They grew rapidly in soil enriched with mushroom compost and mulched with gravel, and within two years they had started to knit together, making a harmoniously coloured dense hedge, several feet high. Six years down the line, pruning them to keep them a manageable size, flowering well, and to maintain a balance between them has proved a simple and satisfying job, carried out at various times from very early spring until late July.

I cut a year's worth of growth off all of those that flower significantly, immediately after they have finished. This is as little as 4–5in (10–13cm) for the daphne, 1–3ft (30–90cm) for the vigorous viburnum, which always needs an extra trim around mid-summer—any later would spoil the following year's flowering. The pittosporums get thinned out and cut about quite robustly if needs be in spring, and may need a further trim a couple of months later. The photinia, a real whopper if left untamed, needs to be reduced by up to a third at least once a year. Because it is sheltered by buildings, I find I can prune it quite hard very early in the season: if the new red shoots get damaged by frost I just snip them off—more are produced within weeks. I trim from time to time throughout the summer, and it keeps on trucking beautifully.

Three years ago I added a little icing to this marvellously rich cake: I planted a viticella clematis, *Clematis* 'Rubra' (also known as *C.* 'Kermesina') nearby. Pruned each spring down to about 3ft (1m), it scrambles around the whole glorious muddle and decorates it with little crimson flowers from mid-summer onwards. Pure heaven.

A ROTTEN LAWN

My small lawn, overshadowed by my neighbour's conifer hedge, is lumpy, mossy and weedy. I have already spent a small fortune on having it improved by professionals but it is no better. I just want a reasonable piece of grass, but am reluctant to throw good money after bad. Can you offer any advice?
Ruth, by email

For every householder who is desperate for the privacy afforded by tall conifers, there is a gardening neighbour next door like you, wringing their hands over miserable grass. As I am sure you know, the problem with this lawn is caused, quite simply, by your neighbour's trees. They are stealing all the light from your grass, leaching out all the nutrients and sucking up all the water from the surrounding soil. Moss and certain weeds are more tolerant than grass of these bad growing conditions and, infuriatingly, the more feeding, watering and pampering you

265

do, the faster the trees will grow and the worse the problem gets.

In an ideal world, you could talk to your neighbour and agree that the trees should be kept at a reasonable height to allow more light into your garden while preserving their privacy. There is legislation to help sort out situations like this: under the Anti-Social Behaviour Act you can ask your local council to judge whether the trees are affecting your enjoyment of your property, but talk first: no council will get involved unless you have tried.

In the meantime, you could take the view that any greenery is better than nothing. Or, if you absolutely must, rake out the moss, and apply a weedkiller in spring. You could then over-seed the area with a shade-tolerant grass seed. But I would advise against spending more money on expensive lawn treatments. If all else fails, give up growing grass there and put a garden bench with its back against your neighbour's trees. Sitting looking at something else may take your mind off things.

LIFE AFTER LEYLANDII

Here's an opposite point of view to Ruth's above. Horrified at the sudden removal (by new neighbours with small children) of a 15ft (5m) well-maintained conifer hedge, Jane and her husband now face the future with an uninterrupted view of one of those lofty, safety-screened trampolines. Is there a hedging plant or tree that they can plant that will grow rapidly to 10–15ft

266

(3–5m) and be easy to maintain? They are so desperate that they are considering planting (gasp!) a new Leylandii hedge.

I fully sympathise about the trampoline. When in use they are inevitably all bobbing heads and squealing and they are impossible to disguise in a small garden. But about the hedge: nothing grows quite as fast as Leylandii, which is why they became the 20th century's boundary fortification of choice—but that is, in my view, no reason to plant another one. Each Leylandii is potentially a huge, greedy tree that may well grow to more than 100ft (30m). The height can be regularly checked (but may need the services of a tree surgeon), but if the width gets out of hand, there's nothing you can do. If you cut back into the old wood, it does not re-shoot, so you are left with an unsightly brown mess. A mature Leylandii hedge creates a huge horticultural no-man's land of dry shade and rooty impoverished soil (see opposite).

It would be far better to plant a mixture of more interesting evergreens. As examples, photinia, green or variegated Portuguese laurel, *Viburnum tinus*, a variegated rhamnus, even a fine-leaved clump-forming bamboo (such as *Fargesia nitida*) are slower growing, true, but will make a much more interesting garden backdrop that can be maintained with secateurs and loppers (see Thank Goodness for Evergreen Shrubs, page 263). Good-sized specimens, planted in rich soil and fed annually, will grow into a pretty mighty hedge in less than five years.

As an alternative, a carefully placed informal group of deciduous trees (or even just a singleton) with fine leaves and twiggy growth will partially hide or efficiently distract the eye away from all sorts of monstrosities in summer. In winter, when the privacy issue is usually not quite so important, it is surprising how much even a tracery of fine bare branches will do a similar job. Trees worth considering are crab apples (such as *Malus floribunda*), the winter-flowering prunus (*Prunus* × *subhirtella* 'Autumnalis'), amelanchier, a twisted willow, as well as some of the birches—best of all is the gorgeous white-stemmed *Betula utilis* var. *jacquemontii*.

Finally a touch of pragmatism. The removal of this hedge may seem like the end of the world for Jane and her husband. But they will find that their garden will, as a result, take on a totally new lease of life, with more air, light and moisture. And of course children grow up, trampolines become obsolete and vanish, new hedges, young trees and other plants will grow to create new interest, fill old gaps. Thankfully we all have an amazing capacity to get used to change, any change—in time.

PRUNING CLIMBING ROSES

Does anyone have climbing roses that look like those illustrated in pruning manuals? Even the ones I have planted myself (as opposed to inheriting/rescuing) don't look particularly businesslike at this time of year, growing—as I like them—in an informal melee with other plants. It is around now that I try to knock them into shape—while they are practically leafless and those last pathetic frosted flowers look about as attractive as a clutch of crumpled paper bags. The good thing about roses is that the more you cut them, the more they grow—you just have to make sure you don't spoil their flower power by cutting off all the wrong stuff.

Start by studying the overall problem. True climbing roses (as opposed to the much more louche and vigorous ramblers; see December, page 235) form a woody framework from which they produce short shoots that flower at the tips from June to December. This framework needs to renew itself, since the best flowers will always be produced on shoots that grow off younger wood. Identify the oldest shoots—thick, dark, woody and probably quite gnarled—and remove at least one from as low down as is practical. This will encourage the rose to make important stout new replacement framework shoots next summer. You may need to snip out the old wood in sections, to avoid damaging younger shoots.

Cut out any bits of dead (brown) wood you can see. Pull down and tie in any good strong, long, new framework shoots that were made last summer and try to get them as horizontal as possible, which encourages them to make flowering side shoots. Do this very gently because by now they may well have stiffened somewhat and be reluctant to bend. If shoots snap off you have only yourself to blame—you should have guided them into position as they developed, so make a mental note for next year. When tying roses, make a twist in the string between the rose branch and the support to prevent chafing.

Next cut right out any thin and feeble growth that would not bear the weight of a flower next year. Roses such as 'Climbing Iceberg' produce

269

masses of this and, once it is removed, the rest of the job becomes much more obvious. You now have to cut back the shoots that have borne flowers (they will probably have hips at the ends unless you picked or deadheaded the flowers during the summer). Cut them back so that two or three leaf scars remain on each shoot, making the cuts close to, and certainly no more than 1/2in (1cm) above, the uppermost scar. You should now be left with a relatively stout, sparse, largely horizontal framework, with a series of neat little green stumps sticking off it, each about 8cm (3in) long. Stand back and make sure that the overall branch pattern is going roughly where it should—you can always re-tie bits or take out more old wood if you are feeling brave. Your rose will probably bear at least a passing resemblance to those daunting illustrations in the pruning books—and it will grow and flower like Billy-oh next season, especially if you feed it with rose food and mulch with well-rotted manure in a few weeks' time.

PRUNING SHRUB ROSES

Several readers are perplexed by their shrub roses, too, wondering when, how and by how much, to prune—or not. Trisha from Chelmsford thinks she might have pruned her beloved 'Fantin-Latour' (a lovely, scented old shrub rose) 'too late', since it produced not a single flower last summer. Meanwhile John wonders whether he can prune his over-large 'Buff Beauty' (a repeat-flowering Hybrid Musk) harder this year to keep it within bounds.

Old shrub roses like Trisha's seem to make cowards of us all and, since they are grown for their innate 'blowsiness', they are too often left to their own devices and barely pruned at all—until they fall off their supports, block paths or only produce their fleeting, powerfully scented mid-summer blooms tantalisingly above nose-height. Maybe this is the fate that befell Trisha's 'Fantin-Latour', and she was forced to prune it too hard, and at the wrong time. Old shrub roses *won't* flower on shoots produced in the current season. They should not, therefore, be cut back in the spring, but should be tackled with care once they have finished flowering—in mid- to late summer— by removing the shoots that have borne flowers, to promote new arching growth that will flower the following year. Then at this time of year, when it is easier to see what is what, they should have their oldest and least productive shoots, those that will have put on the least new top growth, completely removed. Any new shoots subsequently produced from the base (or at least from low down on the remaining framework of branches) may not flower until the following year, and should not be cut back at all until they do.

The modern, repeat-flowering shrub roses (such as 'Buff Beauty' and the popular English Roses) are a different, and easier, kettle of fish altogether. While they have the look and the scent of the old roses, they flower well on shoots produced in the current season and are therefore easier to manage. 'Buff Beauty' is not likely to complain if cut down this spring by a third or even more (not forgetting the removal of any really old or weak wood as well). Hybrid Musks will also flower again particularly profusely in the early autumn if cut back quite hard—by about 2ft (60cm) all over—and fed after their first flush of flowers has finished in July. This might be a way for John to keep his bold six-footer of a rose to a more manageable size.

PALE SKIMMIAS

I have several skimmia plants. Although they are flowering well, the leaves on all but one have turned light yellow over the past few months. We have clay soil. Is this yellowing caused by a deficiency of some sort?
Maureen, by email

Skimmias, leathery-leaved rounded evergreen shrubs which in spring carry panicles of small white or pink heavily scented flowers, are definitely woodland plants and prefer to be grown in dappled shade. Only one variety, the white-flowered *Skimmia* × *confusa* 'Kew Green', is tolerant of full sun. The others may end up with the bleached-out leaves that you describe if they get too much harsh light. This may well be a factor in your case.

Skimmias also prefer leafy, humus-rich soil that is not too alkaline (limey/chalky). If they grow in unsuitable conditions they may be unable to take up nutrients through their roots and can develop iron-deficiency chlorosis, in the same way that camellias do. The leaves become pale between the visible green veins.

If your pale-leaved skimmias are merely getting too much sun you can move them

272

(you could do it now, with care). If you suspect that your soil is 'wrong' for them, then apply an iron tonic (available from garden centres) and perhaps an appropriate controlled-release fertiliser suitable for acid-loving plants, topped with a mulch of composted bark or leaf mould.

HELLEBORE LEAVES

When should I cut back the leaves of my hellebores? Or should I not cut them back at all, but leave them to protect the new flowers and leaves from frost?
Eva, by email

It depends which kind of hellebores you are referring to. The leaves of the showy oriental hybrids (highly prized for their long-stemmed white, cream, pink or plum-coloured flowers in early spring) should indeed get the chop around now. Last year's huge leaves will be looking tired and flat, and very possibly diseased. If they are removed now the new flowers will look all the more spectacular against the bare soil (or, even better, with a backdrop of freshly applied leaf mould or compost mulch), emerging as they do just before a brand new shiny crop of leaves.

Removal of old leaves also ensures that any young seedlings that are dotted around have a better chance of survival and rapid growth, by letting the rain and air get into the area. Oriental hybrid hellebores set seed and multiply quite easily. They won't flower, of

273

course, for a year or two. If you are fussy about their colour, you can often tell which seedlings are going to have dark leaves and flowers even when they are in their infancy, by the colour of their minute stems.

Even in the nastiest of winters, hellebores are completely hardy. This fact was brought home to me when I saw swathes of *Helleborus corsicus* (now renamed *H. argutifolius*) flowering merrily only just below the tree line amid patches of snow in their native Corsica a few years ago. But these, along with other species such as *H.* × *sternii* and *H. foetidus*, produce flowers in the tips of the almost shrubby shoots they make during the previous growing season. If they were to be cut down now, all would be lost. The best treatment is a mid-summer clean-up: if you completely remove all the tatty shoots that have flowered, the whole plant will look better and you will make room for fresh stems to power upward, ready to flower the following spring.

Incidentally, if you thought that the only way to appreciate hellebore flowers was either to bend down and tip their frustratingly downward-cast 'faces' up momentarily, or by resorting to decapitating them and floating them in water, here's a tip sent in by a doctor in Abingdon. I tried it and it works extremely well.

To stop hellebores from flopping as cut flowers, fill a washing-up bowl with water, place the cut stem in the water held in your left hand (if right handed) and crush the stem firmly between thumb and forefinger, about

1½in (4cm) above the cut. Then with a pair of scissors, still under water, cut through the crushed area. This removes an airlock in the stem, and almost immediately the new cut end of the flower stem stiffens and splays out slightly, and can be transferred to a vase.

KILLER IVY?

My hedge has ivy growing through it. I have been warned that it will kill off the hedge and that I should cut it out. Does ivy really kill trees and hedges?
Denis, by email

Ivy does not actually kill trees—it is not a parasitic plant. The little roots it puts out along the length of its climbing stems are for clinging, not feeding. However, once it has climbed up into the tree canopy, the trouble really starts. Its growth changes in character, it becomes shrubby and starts to flower, forming an evergreen, bulky addition to the tree. In time this makes the tree top heavy and less able to cope with strong wind. It is always advisable to take steps to stop ivy getting into the canopies of old trees by frequently severing any stems that start to climb. The results are unsightly—you just have to wait for the old brown leaves to fall away naturally, by which time fresh ivy stems will be making every attempt to take their place. It is a constant battle.

With hedges, the problem is slightly different. Ivy will frequently scramble around in the base of a healthy hedge, but seldom kills it. An annual grapple, rip and hack will generally keep things under control. However, where individual hedge plants die back because of old age or honey fungus, the ivy will quickly take over, climb into the skeletal remains and fill the gap, actually forming quite a solid part of the hedge itself. In certain circumstances this can actually be useful—where replacement of the section of hedge would be too difficult to contemplate.

There are no rights and wrongs about ivy. People either love it or hate it. It does, however, provide important cover for birds and other wildlife, and a breeding ground for butterflies.

STOOLING, COPPICING AND POLLARDING

I am reluctant to display my ignorance, but could you explain the difference between pollarding, stooling and coppicing?
J A, by email

Stooling and coppicing are just different words for the same thing, namely the cutting down to the base (or in the case of trees, to a very short trunk) of woody plants every so often, in order to control their size. After stooling or coppicing, trees such as eucalyptus, catalpa and paulownia become multi-stemmed and may produce massive or more attractive leaves. Ornamental garden shrubs with colourful young growth also benefit—the most obvious being ruby-stemmed cornus (dogwood) and willows. For example, the beautiful willow variety with winter-scarlet young stems and a mouthful of a name: *Salix alba* var. *vitellina* 'Britzensis'. Coppicing is a tradition that is as old as time. In my part of the country, the High Weald, much of the woodland consists of chestnut trees that were repeatedly coppiced to provide long, straight hop poles.

Pollarding is similar in that it involves the dramatic reduction and control of growth of trees (in late winter or early spring), but leaving a tall trunk. Pollarding was frequently carried out on street trees such as lime and London plane to prevent them outgrowing their space, and results in the knobbly top growth with which we are all familiar. But many other larger trees such as ash and sycamore respond well to the treatment too. Pollarding has to be done regularly—every few years—to prevent dangerous top-heavy growth, and is best carried out by qualified tree surgeons.

February

TO MULCH OR NOT TO MULCH?

Well, that's January done with. By the middle of this month we will notice the days are lengthening just a touch and—with inevitable frosty setbacks—the great annual garden merry-go-round will get under way again. It is time for the seriously conscientious to start barrowing in the muck and mulches.

It is easy to feel envious of those immaculate spring gardens where every inch of visible soil is covered in a thick, weed-smothering duvet of organic stuff, but joined-up wall-to-wall mulching is not really my thing. I like my common-or-garden plants to self-seed freely, and thick mulching would rather knock this on the head. I positively enjoy a froth of forget-me-nots turning up in unexpected places (although I don't put the spent plants in the compost heap for fear of infesting it with seeds); I welcome 'unplanned' crowds of bright white honesty or yellow and orange Welsh poppies rising up out of a seemingly undisciplined self-sown carpet of Bowles' golden grass. In my former rural garden, I was even more lenient. I used to positively encourage (shock horror) weedy ox-eye daisies and even cow parsley to embellish certain areas of my borders. In my opinion (and that, really, was the only one that mattered...) they looked fabulous in an all green-and-white bed in dappled shade, along with blue-ish and stripy-leaved hostas.

278

So rather than an annual spring compost splurge, gentle soil improvement in my garden goes on more or less all the time. I dig compost into the soil as I plant and as I split perennials or move things around. I mulch individual perennial clumps this month and—hawk-eyed, looking out for emerging bulbs and young seedlings—I spread as thick a layer as I dare of fine leaf mould in between them, tickling it into the top inch or so of soil. This week I navigated my way around an abundance of honesty seedlings, culling 'extras' as I went, and noticed the first minuscule skinny little seedlings of 'Mother of Pearl' poppies and foxgloves were beginning to show up. This kind of gardening is much more time-consuming than applying the duvet, but, in my view, the results are worth the efforts.

Mind you, I am as tough as the next gardener with real thugs. And while in my old garden I fought in vain to control ground elder and bindweed, I absolutely pounced on other weeds—particularly nettles, brambles that invaded from the farm hedges and rashes of thistles, seeds of which blew in from an adjacent unkempt field. After some years toiling in my tidy new village garden I still find rosettes of hairy bittercress (the horror that flowers, seeds and germinates all year round), dock seedlings and, here and there, rapidly spreading mats of willow herb.

OXALIS: AN ORNAMENTAL THAT BECAME A NUISANCE

Two kinds of oxalis drive gardeners to distraction. First there is the little perennial bulb-forming species, *Oxalis debilis*, with pink flowers, originally imported as an ornamental plant and now a major irritating (but, it has to be said, not other-plant-threatening) weed. Little shamrock-like leaves pop up everywhere from immature bulbils, and these are best tackled in spring, while still 'green'. I have used a kitchen fork for this somewhat thankless job, putting the resulting gleanings firmly in the dustbin. If you delay the job till autumn, the bulbs will have become fragile and explosive, and will scatter far and wide as you work, making the problem worse the following spring. Applying a permanent, very thick mulch will eventually obliterate this weed. In the absence of this, I find that turning a blind eye is pretty effective, too.

The other oxalis (*Oxalis corniculata*) is a creeping, spreading menace with similar-shaped leaves and little yellow flowers followed by explosive seeds. The best treatment in flowerbeds is to fork it out before it flowers and seeds or carefully treat it with glyphosate. It is particularly hideous if it invades lawns since it is resistant to selective lawn weedkillers. You can try raking it out in early autumn, but you may have to live with it for ever unless you are prepared to weedkill the lawn and start again.

CELANDINES IN THE WRONG PLACE

Claire from Faversham, Kent, has got a really nasty problem popping up all over the borders in her new garden. She sent me a sample to see if I could identify it and suggest a remedy. What she sent me were celandine leaves, and I don't envy her one bit. Celandines are positively lovely in the right place, in hedgerows and wild areas of a garden, forming ground-hugging mats of little round, green leaves in late winter. Undisturbed clumps produce masses of starry yellow flowers that open right up in the early spring sunshine, and are a marvellous sight. There is even a bronze-leaved one that is to be seen regularly for sale in garden centres.

One of the reasons celandines in the wrong place are hard to eradicate is the fact that they go completely dormant in mid-summer. You can simply forget that they are there. The little bulbs are brown, and virtually undetectable in the soil—which makes it really hard a) to dig them out and b) not to inadvertently spread them all over the place while you are trying to do so.

The best course of action would be to paint or spray isolated clumps very carefully with glyphosate weedkiller when they are at their leafiest in a few weeks' time. Take care to protect any other emerging plants from contact with the chemical. Alternatively, scoop off the top layer of soil—the bulbs will be close to the surface—and get rid of it. Again, this should be done while you can still see the extent of the problem.

AN 'INFESTATION' OF SNOWDROPS?

I have to say, this is not a collective noun I would use, but Jill from Ipswich says she has allowed the ground under deciduous trees in her garden to become 'infested' with snowdrops in spring. The area, which Jill sees from that important vantage point, the kitchen sink, is rather bare for the rest of the year. Are there low-maintenance plants that would liven it up later on, but cope with the relative summer gloom?

The problem is not just summer gloom, but summer drought—the soil will obviously be rather dry under the trees in summer, and most plants or colonies of plants will need a little 'high-maintenance' help to get established. That said, there are plants that will spread around quite easily under trees with the snowdrops: *Euphorbia amygdaloides* var. *robbiae*, a creeping evergreen spurge, is one and a small-leaved variegated periwinkle (*Vinca minor* 'Argenteovariegata') is another. But be warned: both of these useful ground-cover species can develop thug-like tendencies if allowed to be too 'low maintenance', however.

Hardy autumn- to spring-flowering cyclamen will colonise under trees, as will oriental hybrid hellebores (on sale in flower now, so that you can choose colours you like), which would provide some dramatic, virtually evergreen foliage, too. But taking a leaf from my own book, by (rather lazily) simply looking up from my desk and out of my window: in a shady part of my own garden is a small area colonised by biennial white honesty— the variety with variegated leaves is one I

282

particularly like in shade. Its early summer flowers produce silver-papery seed heads that are still attractive months later, caught in a shaft of sunlight as I write. Another good-value plant is a clump-forming, drought- and shade-tolerant aster, surprisingly not more often grown: *Aster divaricatus*. In summer it produces a cloud of small white daisy flowers on wiry blackish stems. These then have a long-lasting bronze/brown winter presence—even now, as the New Year's growth is starting, I am loath to cut them down.

FUNGUS GNATS

For the past three years the bulb fibre in which I grow my hyacinth bulbs seems to have become the breeding ground for extremely small flies. Do you know what they are, and is there a way of killing the flies without damaging the bulbs?
J B, Morpeth, Northumberland

These are undoubtedly some form of fungus gnat, also known as sciarid fly. There are many different species, the larvae of which feed on decayed plant material and fungi in soil and are attracted to composts with high organic content. Most of them are harmless to plants, but they can become more noticeable and rather irritating in confined spaces, and they can easily go on breeding all year round in heated greenhouses.

You can control fungus gnats by watering a solution of an insecticide containing imidacloprid into the soil around your bulbs, which will clobber the tiny white larvae.

Another solution that might nip the problem in the bud, as it were, would be to cover the compost in your hyacinth pots with a layer of coarse sand or grit about ½in (1cm) thick, which will discourage the adult flies from laying eggs there in the first place.

SEEING SPOTS

Last autumn I removed a branch of our 15-year-old acer that had shed its leaves and died during a summer heat wave. I noticed recently that an orange-coloured mould had appeared on the remains of the branch and seems to be travelling further down the tree. Should I do more pruning—take out another branch or so? Can I spray the tree to save it, or are its days numbered?
Elizabeth, by email

This is a classic attack by a fungus called, appropriately, coral spot (*Nectria cinnabarina*), to which acers and many other woody garden plants—including currants and gooseberries—are particularly susceptible. It can also attack completely dead wood, even old softwood garden furniture and garden gates, and is extremely hard to eradicate. The fungus generally gets hold of plants via pruning cuts or dead, injured sections of branches, particularly if they are constantly damp. Once there it can spread through the plant, causing the wilting and die back, branch by branch, that you experienced.
    You should most certainly prune out the

284

affected parts of the tree, cutting back at least 6in (15cm) below the lowest orange spots. Immediately thereafter you should spray the tree with a fungicide and repeat this at three-weekly intervals—and clean your secateurs. Since acers are such a prime target for this disease, you should keep an eye open for the orange spots or pustules in the future—they often appear in early spring.

As a rule, you can keep this creeping little nasty at bay by being reasonably tidy around the garden—clearing up all your woody prunings and snippings, etc. Burn or dispose of any plant material already infected.

PLANTS FOR A TROUGH

We would like to plant up an old water trough. It is 12ft (3.7m) long, 18in (45cm) high and wide, set on bricks against an east-facing wall that loses the sun in the afternoons. Have you any ideas? What do we do about drainage?
Julia, Chichester, Sussex

You don't say so, but I presume this is an old iron farm trough. I have one similar, though not as long, and have made it into a small 'pond' with marginals planted in large fabric pond pots standing in the water.

Since there is no drainage and you are understandably unwilling or unable to make holes in the base of this mighty container, you would do best to find a way of using plants that require permanently wet feet. Rather than a pond, you could make the trough into

285

a long, narrow bog garden. With a bit of ingenuity you could even have a simple and low-key circulating water feature at one end or in the middle, to break up its length. Some sort of rustic old pipe or tap on the wall, with a pump and a small reservoir such as a black garden bucket perhaps, sunk into the compost, topped with a metal mesh piled with stones would do the trick.

In order to create the boggy planting part you will have to put about 4in (10cm) of rubble in the bottom of the trough as a rudimentary drainage layer, then line it with an off-cut of pond liner punctured in a few places. This will retain moisture and protect roots from the rusty iron of the container. The planting medium should be a mixture of ericaceous compost and weed-free topsoil with about 15 per cent added lime-free grit. Even with a root depth of roughly 1ft (30cm) you will still get some height and colour in the summer months with variegated-leaved yellow irises, giant rhubarb-like rheums, blue *Pontederia cordata* and scarlet *Lobelia cardinalis* and various rushes and sedges. The edges of the trough and any visible underpinnings of the rustic faucet affair could be softened by trailing carpets of creeping Jenny and water forget-me-not. The whole caboodle will attract loads of wildlife, will need to be kept well watered in summer and may have to be overhauled every two or three years.

SHRUB/CLIMBER COMBINATION

I have a passion flower growing on a fence, but it wants to climb all over adjacent plants. I am particularly concerned about my ceanothus— about 5ft (1.5m) high and wide. Will the passion flower kill it?
Andrea, by email

There is always bound to be a slight conflict of interests where shrubs and climbers are concerned. Climbers were, after all, invented before anyone thought of gardening and fences, and their means of climbing—twining, clinging or, in the case of passion flowers, using little springy tendrils—were designed specifically for using other plants as a means to getting upwards to the sun.

Your passion flower/ceanothus combination could just about work well with a little bit of vigilance. As I've mentiond before, passion flowers grow best in this country if they are pruned fairly hard each year in late spring—even down to within 2ft (60cm) of the ground. If you don't do this, they tend to go on growing from where they left off the previous year, while the old growth just hangs there looking moth-eaten and straggly. I would now cut yours back by about half—which may well remove some of the growth that is festooning your ceanothus while not exposing the bottom of the passion flower to possible frost, and then cut it back again properly when spring well and truly arrives. The ceanothus (you don't say which variety, but I am presuming it is an evergreen spring-flowerer) will need to have its old flowering shoots nipped back by 1ft (30cm) or so in June—so until then you should try to keep the passion flower's new young growth confined to the fence. Once you have pruned, you can let everything do its own thing—the ceanothus should be just about tough enough to cope with a limited late summer invasion like this every year.

Some climber/woody plant combinations just don't work at all because their pruning needs are completely at odds with each other. The classic impossible mish-mash combination is that of early flowering clematis (such as 'Nelly Moser' and co) and climbing roses.

DECKING ANYONE?

At last! People may be waking up to the fact that the combination of decking and the murky British winter is not, to say the least, a marriage made in heaven. Hopefully the fad for obliterating perfectly lovely little green back gardens under great boring swathes of it may start to decline. In its second year and beyond, once that slick garden-makeover newness has faded and proud owners have become bored with sweeping and power washing and generally slapping it about with smelly and expensive unguents, gardens full of decking can quickly become hideously slippery and frequently slimy no-go areas for most of the winter. Emailers Carolyn (who inherited hers) and Rosanne (who really likes hers—in summer) are just two sadly challenged 'deckists' wondering how to get around the problem. Rosanne has coped with winter wet by spreading sand on her deck, which, she says, helps a bit—but at the same time defeating the whole object of having all that nice permanently clean surface under foot by making a mess in its own right, I should have thought. Have I any ideas? Well, there are some non-toxic products on the market and I suppose this gives me an opportunity to extol the considerable virtues of Biotal Algae and Mould Stain Cleaner—a plant-friendly, colourless and odourless water-soluble liquid that, with a single application via broom, bucket and a little bit of effort, will see off the slime from wood, paving stones and garden furniture for several months. But I realise that decking is slippery even if it isn't green with algae, so what then? Galvanised chicken wire, neatly stapled down over the treacherous bits, at least makes a safe pathway across it. But please, can we get back to real gardening? In my view, scrubbing decking just isn't. Harrumph.

POTTING COMPOSTS

Rather than buying bagged composts, Malcolm would like to make his own compost in which to germinate seeds this year. What is the simplest way to do this? Can he use the soil thrown up by the busy moles in his orchard mixed with some garden compost?

Malcolm could make a reasonable compost suitable for germinating seeds by mixing 2 parts mole-hill soil to 1 part sand and 1 part sieved leaf mould or fine, perfectly rotted garden compost.

Mole-hill soil may be relatively 'clean', but he should be aware that both ordinary garden topsoil and garden compost may not be completely weed-free.

As plants grow, they need a stronger growing medium that has a greater mineral and nutrition content, so he should alter the ratio to about 7 parts soil, 3 parts garden compost or leaf mould and 2 parts sand. To this he could add some slow-release fertiliser pellets.

Frank writes to say that he happily uses ready-mixed composts out of a bag and wants to know if these have a 'shelf life', since he has half a bag left over from last year. He does not say what kind of compost he uses, and there are now loads on the market for every kind of plant, so I can only write in the most general terms. As long as the bags are stored in a cool, dry place, they should be fine to use after a year, although some suppliers state that the nutrient content can deteriorate after that. The main enemy is wet. Most compost bags seem to have a line of small perforations in them, so if stored flat, outside and unprotected for a long time, the contents easily become saturated and will deteriorate. So buy bagged composts from a supplier with a high turnover, store them under cover and use them within a year or two.

A BURNING QUESTION

I would like to use the ash from my wood-burning stove on the garden. How should I store the ash and for how long, or can I just mix it into the compost heap?
Jackie, Ash (yes really!), near Canterbury, Kent

Ash from a wood-burner is very slightly alkaline, but has relatively little value as a fertiliser (bonfire ash has slightly more). Unlike general bonfire ash, which tends to be more gritty because of the mixed origin of its components (soily roots and so on), logs burn away extremely efficiently in a wood-burner and the resulting ash is powdery and lacking in substance, becoming slimy when wet. If your burner produces ash with some substance to it, you could dig some of it into your garden to help break down clay soil—if you have it. Coarser wood ash can also be used as a slug/snail barrier around young plants. By all means store some of your ash (in a dry place), and add a little at a time to your compost heap, particularly in summer when you are composting more greenery in the form of lawn clippings, prunings and snippings, and the rotting activity in the heap accelerates somewhat. I should love to tell you that your wood-burning stove produces a wonderful, free and magic gardening by-product—but, alas, it doesn't.

MOULDY CUTTINGS

I successfully took penstemon cuttings in the summer, overwintering them in pots in a cold frame covered with a double layer of fleece. I have noticed that quite a few have developed mildew. Will they recover as the weather improves? Will the mould spread?
Moira, by email

This is botrytis, a particularly nasty mould that tends to take hold when growing conditions are damp and airless. You should remove any dead plants and those plants that look too far gone to recover, and snip away any even slightly damaged foliage from others. The fungus can indeed spread to other susceptible plants in your cold frame— soft-stemmed plants such as pelargoniums seem to go down like nine-pins. Control with fungicides is difficult, but rather than do nothing you could (on a mild day) take out all the plants from your cold frame, pick off dead, damaged or diseased foliage, and spray the entire plant population (including, for good measure, the compost in the pots) with a systemic fungicide. Most importantly, on future mild days open up your cold frame to keep the air circulating and generally dry out the atmosphere in there.

While we're on the subject of penstemons, don't cut back established garden plants yet. However much of a battering all that rather brittle 'evergreen' top growth received during bad weather, it still protects the new growth around the base of each plant. It is these tiny shoots that will bear the coming summer's flowers—not the longer old stems that should be cut down in the spring. The further north you live, obviously, the later you should leave jobs like this: late short sharp frosts can be the very plague for marginally tender plants—and for impatient gardeners, anxious to clean up the premises 'ready for the off'.

BEST MANURE

Is there a difference in the essential qualities of horse manure when the horses are standing on wood chips as opposed to straw?
W A, by email

Horse manure combined with wood chips breaks down into useful fertilising material for gardeners far more slowly than that combined with straw—or even hemp fibre or hop waste, which is also common nowadays as horse bedding. Consequently the wood-chip manure is generally recommended as a top dressing or a mulch, while straw or other manure is excellent as a soil conditioner, adding foody bulk to both light and sandy soil or heavy clay soils and everything in between.

The general rot rule applies to all manures: if it still smells nasty, it is too young. 'Fresh' manure can burn plant roots and stems, and needs to be left to mature, preferably under cover, for at least six months.

GENERAL FERTILISERS

What exactly is a 'general fertiliser'? I use blood, fish and bone, but in my country garden it seems to drive the local wildlife mad, and I find my new plantings dug up and scattered everywhere. Is there something else similar that I could use?
Verity, Presteigne, Powys

This is a big boffiny subject, but I will try to put it as simply as possible. A general fertiliser is one that is 'balanced'—that is, one that has more or less equal quantities of the three macronutrients essential for plant growth. These are nitrogen (N), vital for good green leaf growth); phosphorus (P), essential for root health and development; and potassium (K) to encourage maximum flower and fruit production. Blood, fish and bone is the general fertiliser of choice for organic gardeners. Pelleted chicken manure is an organic alternative to blood, fish and bone fertiliser but is more variable, and the brand I have been using certainly has a slightly higher nitrogen content. Oddly enough, when I had a similar problem in my old garden I changed to chicken manure, which surprisingly perhaps did not drive the local foxes wild. There are inorganic general fertilisers available too—look for them at your garden centre—and if you check on the back of the packaging of all plant foods, you will see the NPK ratio listed. And there are special fertilisers for specific jobs: spring lawn fertiliser, for example, has high nitrogen content; autumn lawn food has high phosphorus content while tomato food is high in potassium.

SPOTS ON ACER BRANCHES

There are white, woolly-edged spots on the underside of the branches and on the sunless side of the trunk of my acer. I presume this is a

fungal infection of some sort. The tree is 25–30 years old and is approximately 25ft (7.5m) tall. Growth or leaves do not appear to be affected. Any help you can give in identifying this problem will be appreciated.
Chris, by email

I think it's likely that this is not a fungal disease but an infestation of scale insects, specifically the horse chestnut scale (*Pulvinaria regalis*), which plagues various large trees; horse chestnuts, as the name suggests, sycamores and limes, as well as ornamental acers, magnolias, cornus and bay trees. Heavy infestations are quite alarming looking and most noticeable in summer, but the tiny beasts are unlikely to disfigure the foliage or even harm the tree to any great degree. This is just as well, since realistically there is not much that can be done about getting rid of scale insects on a tree this size. You could brush off some of the visible immobile 'spots'—mature females—and later on spray as much of the tree as you can reach with a winter wash. This is a traditional technique for getting rid of pests that overwinter on trees; original washes were tar-oil-based but this is now banned. You should be able to find an organic alternative such as Growing Success Winter Wash online or at the garden centre.

GERANIUM CUTTINGS

On the advice of a friend I pinched out the tips of some of the geranium cuttings I had successfully taken last autumn. Soon afterwards the larger of their remaining leaves turned red and wilted. I am disappointed since they had been such healthy plants. What has caused this—over-watering/under-watering? Or is it something to do with the pinching out?
Mary, by email

I suppose over-watering is a possibility, but I think it is unlikely that you have under-watered your geranium (strictly speaking, pelargonium) cuttings, which—once they have 'taken'—are quite happy to spend the winter almost bone dry. I routinely abandon mine on the windowsill of my garage until around the beginning of March, when the process of resurrecting them begins.

Reading between the lines of your email, I suspect that when you took cuttings last autumn you took quite long mature shoots from the parent plants and left the leaves on them. It is these old leaves that have now turned red and look rather sad. They would have dropped off around now even if you had not pinched out the growing tips. Instead of just pinching out those tips you would have done better to reduce them to almost lifeless stumps about 2–3in (5–8cm) tall—as you would do to the parent plant had you overwintered it—and then started to water sparingly a week or two ago. They would by now have been putting out masses of new growth. You could still do this (presuming you have not given up on them altogether), and although it might seem a bit brutal, if they have good roots, your plants will soon catch up with everything else and can be potted on soon after.

To avoid this problem in future years, take your cuttings from short, young shoots, cutting just below a node (leaf joint), removing any tiny flower buds that are in evidence in the shoot tips, together with all but one or two leaves.

Directory of Suppliers

Many of the products mentioned in the text are available from your local garden centre. If you can't find a stockist for a specific product, consult the list below.

Bayer Fungus Fighter; Bayer Tree Stump Killer; for stockists go to bayergarden.co.uk and click on 'where to buy'

Biotal Algae and Mould Stain Cleaner; Biotal Compost Maker; available from the Organic Gardening Catalogue (OrganicCatalogue.com 0845 130 1304)

Bosch electric shredders; for more information go to bosch-pt.co.uk/gardentools

Canvas kneelers from The Carrier Company carriercompany.co.uk 01328 820699

Cheshunt Compound from Bayer, see above

Chiltern Seeds, Bortree Stile, Ulverston, Cumbria chilternseeds.co.uk

Composted bark from Gardenscape gardenscapedirect.co.uk 0800 854 663, will deliver in the south-east

Copper snail tape and copper pot feet from greengardener.co.uk

Copperbed slug and snail barrier paint from copperbed.co.uk 0845 2252118

Dandelion trowel and other Sneeboer hand tools from harrodhorticultural.com 0845 402 5300

Darlac compost stirrer, 01753 547 790 for stockists or email info@darlac.com

Deer protection black plastic netting from harrodhorticultural.com 0845 402 5300

EcoCharlie Natural Slug and Snail Deterrent from ecocharlie.co.uk 01798 867 780

Enviromat sedum matting from enviromat.co.uk 01842 828 266

Felco tools from worldoffelco.co.uk 0208 829 8850

Flexi-Tie go to flexi-tie.co.uk and click on 'stockists'

Glyphosate weedkillers (e.g. Roundup, Tumbleweed) from amazon.co.uk

Growing Success Advanced Slug Killer from organiccatalog.com

Just Green Ice Free for Bird Baths from just-green.com 01621 785088

Maxicrop go to maxicrop.co.uk and click on 'where to buy Maxicrop' 08700 115117

Nemaslug Slug Killer and Nemasys Vine Weevil Killer go to nemasysinfo.com and click on 'buy products' for stockists

NGS gardens open for charity ngs.org.uk 01483 211535

Pro-Grow compost pro-grow.co.uk or call CPL on 0800 3286693 cpldistribution.co.uk.

Provado Ultimate Bug Killer; Provado Vine Weevil Killer; from Bayer see above

Rootgrow mycorrhizal fungi from plantworksuk.co.uk

Rootrainers from haxnicks.co.uk

Scott's Liquid Slugclear from gardenshop.telegraph.co.uk

Slug Buggers from greengardener.co.uk

Slug Shocka copper fabric from greengardener.co.uk

SnailAway electric fence from electricfencingsolutions.co.uk

Socusil from Doff from choiceful.com

Sulphurlawn from greenacresdirect.co.uk

Systhane Fungus Fighter from Bayer, see above

Usual and Unusual Plants, Onslow House, Magham Down, Hailsham, Sussex BN27 1PL; uuplants.co.uk 01323 840967

Vitax Conifer and Shrub Fertiliser go to vitax.co.uk and click on 'where to buy'

Weedol weedkiller order from amazon.co.uk

Wilkinson pruning saw from choiceful.com

Winter Tree Wash (organic) from greengardener.co.uk

Information correct at time of going to press.

Acknowledgements

First, of course, I would like to thank my editors at *Telegraph* Gardening for planting the seeds of the Thorny Problems page, and encouraging them to flourish with minimal snipping about over the years. It was Tiffany Daneff who took me on as a comparative novice, but subsequent editors Kylie O'Brien and Joanna Fortnam, who were at various times assisted by Harriet Lane-Fox and Claudine Beaumont, have all been immensely encouraging. I am grateful, too, to Caroline Buckland, Head of Books and Entertainment at Telegraph Media Group, who championed the idea of making the book out of Thorny Problems and found just the right publisher. They have without exception been a pleasure to work with.

Having to prune Thorny Problems down to a manageable size for a book was a bit of a nightmare. I have to thank my son Henry without whose initial technical help and constant encouragement I would probably still be dithering about over my laptop wondering where to start. But for the real editing, I am utterly indebted to Sharon Amos, for the brilliant job she has done converting a mass of material into something sensible and readable, to the illustrator Sophie Allport and to Francine Lawrence and all those at Simon & Schuster who have managed to create a lovely-looking book of which we can all be proud.

I should also like to acknowledge here the help I have received from experts and specialists who have enabled me to fill in gaps in my knowledge and experience, and so answer readers' questions more helpfully. Guy Barter and his team at the Royal Horticultural Society Advisory Service have always been incredibly generous with their time and advice, as have horticultural suppliers, growers and manufacturers of all sorts. Along the way I have learnt an awful lot and I am immensely grateful to them all.

Of course, there would be no Thorny Problems without the thousands of *Telegraph* readers who have written to me, trusting me to give them constructive answers to their gardening problems—however odd or mundane those problems may be. So they deserve my heartfelt thanks, too. Through the murk of angst and uncertainty in their letters has shone a glorious passion for their own gardens and for gardening in general, along with genuine down-to-earth humour and goodwill, which I hope I have passed on through my writing.